Land Here? You Bet!

Land Here? You Bet!

The True Adventures of a Fledgling Bush Pilot in Alaska and British Columbia in the Early 1950s

Sunny Fader and Edward (Ted) Huntley

Ketchikan

Sullivan
Bay

Seattle

hancock

house

ISBN 0-88839-557-0

Cataloging in Publication Data

Fader, Sunny, 1931–
    Land here? you bet! : the true adventures of a fledgling bush
pilot in Alaska and British Columbia in the early 1950s / Sunny
Fader and Edward (Ted) Huntley.

    ISBN 0-88839-550-7

    1. Fader, Sunny, 1931–. 2. Bush pilots—Alaska—Biography.
3. Bush pilots—British Columbia—Biography.
I. Huntley, Edward (Ted), 1930–1996 II. Title.

TL540.H86A3 2005   629.13'092   C2003-911255-1

Printed in South Korea — PACOM
Editor: Margaret Jetelina
Production: Genevieve MacKay, Ingrid Luters
Photographs: Edward Huntley collection unless otherwise credited.
Map, page 2-3: Walt Green and Rick Emaus

Published simultaneously in Canada and the United States by

HANCOCK HOUSE PUBLISHERS LTD.
19313 Zero Avenue, Surrey, B.C. V3S 9R9
(604) 538-1114 Fax (604) 538-2262

HANCOCK HOUSE PUBLISHERS
1431 Harrison Avenue, Blaine, WA 98230-5005
(604) 538-1114 Fax (604) 538-2262
Web Site: www.hancockhouse.com *email:* sales@hancockhouse.com

Contents

Edward (Ted) Huntley
1930 – 1996

Preface

There are many reasons for writing a book: to tell a story, to make the reader smile, to share information, to impart wisdom. Hopefully, this book will do all of these things. But the real reason I sought to have *Land Here? You Bet!* published is to pay tribute to a special friend, Ted Huntley. Ted was a man who not only knew how to follow his own dreams, but who had a gift for helping others find in themselves the courage and commitment to follow their dreams. Although he is no longer with us, I hope that this recounting of his tales as a bush pilot in the 1950s will allow him to continue to inspire others.

I am not sure if it was the power of Ted's vision, the force of his personality or his contagious zest for living, but most people who knew him saw him as someone who epitomized the aphorism "bigger than life." He certainly seemed that way to me when I met him in June 1991 while looking for a place to live on Bainbridge Island, a small community just a ferry ride away from Seattle, Washington.

By then Ted had retired from his job as a captain for Delta Air Lines and owned a unique company that leased reworked wooden tugboats to organizations engaged in scientific research. He had always loved those old wooden tugs. He got the idea to revamp them when he learned that the metal in modern boats interfered with some of the sophisticated electronic instruments marine scientists used in their work. Since flying continued to be his greatest passion, his company also offered its clients air support when needed.

When I went house hunting on Bainbridge that summer, Ted and his wife, Nancy, and their two young children, Chris and Annie, had just settled into a new home, a waterfront compound on Puget Sound with ample room for their menagerie of dogs, cats, horses and one friendly mountain goat. Fortunately for me, the property also had a wonderful little two-bedroom cabin on it in need of a tenant. Tucked away in the trees, with a big stone fireplace, beach access, and a view of the stable and horse pasture, it was just the kind of place I was looking for.

I was surprised when the Huntleys greeted my confession that I was a freelance writer with enthusiasm. Such an admission sends up a red flag to most landlords: erratic income, unpaid rent, etc. I found out some months later that the night before they began interviewing potential tenants, Ted and Nancy both agreed that the cabin was perfect for a writer. If they could find a writer, Nancy hoped that perhaps he (or she) would help Ted, an inveterate storyteller, get some of the wonderful stories of his years of flying down on paper.

My goal in moving to the Northwest was to semi-retire and pursue my long coveted dream of becoming an author. For forty years I had made my living, first, as a journalist, then as a film and television writer, but what I had always wanted to do was write books. My faith in my ability to accomplish this, however, was somewhat tenuous. That is, until I met Ted. Ted reacted to my passion for writing a book with such enthusiasm that I soon found myself believing not only that it was possible, but that it would be impossible for me not to accomplish this. Mentoring came as naturally to him as breathing.

Over time, Ted and Nancy and I became friends. I loved listening to Ted's flying stories, and he loved telling them, so I suppose it was inevitable that at some time my dream and Ted's desire to document his experiences would come together. Exactly whose idea it was to collaborate, I do not remember. The project just seemed to evolve.

The book we agreed to work on together, by Ted's choice, was not to be about him, but about some of the colorful characters he had come to know during his career. Ted began taping his recollections. I transcribed the tapes and developed the information into stories, which he reviewed for accuracy, adding any additional information he remembered. The process seemed to be working. We managed to put three chapters together, and my agent found a publisher who expressed some interest in the proposed book. However, the publisher first wanted to see a chapter about the man who was telling the stories.

At first Ted was reluctant. While he was willing, even eager, to relate his experiences, his focus was always on the other people involved. I suspect his Scandinavian heritage, a culture that tends to foster reserve, had something to do with this. Finally, we came up with a compromise. He agreed to make a tape about how he became a bush pilot. This would introduce the reader to him, but would also give him the opportunity to pay tribute to others.

In 1996, the week before Easter, Ted gave me the new tapes and headed off to Pascagoula, Mississippi, full of enthusiasm about a groundbreaking venture he had just put together involving a revolutionary new airborne laser mapping system. That was the last time I saw him. On April 7—Easter Sunday—Ted died of a massive heart attack.

I was devastated. Ted had become a major part of my life. More than just a good friend, he was my muse, my motivator, the slayer of my doubts. I owed him so much. I would have liked to finish the book we were working on as a tribute to him, but without him and more stories I knew that was impossible. So I put all the tapes and manuscript pages away.

A month or so after his death, Nancy arranged a memorial service for Ted at the Museum of Flight at Boeing Field in Seattle. It was to be a celebration of his life. Friends came from all over the country. There was even a gentleman there who had flown in from his home in London. They each had their own special "Ted story." Some stories were funny, some poignant, but most were about how Ted had given the teller the courage to pursue his or her dreams. Clearly, just as he had been a pivotal force in my life, helping me to inaugurate positive change, he had served that same role in many other lives.

When I got home that day, I took out the last three tapes Ted had recorded, which I had not yet listened to. I hadn't been able to. But now I hungered to hear my old friend's voice. What I heard when I played those tapes was not the voice of the sixty-seven-year-old man I had known. It was as though the twenty-year-old inside him had come to life as he recounted the two summers in the early 1950s when he finally realized his boyhood dream ... the two summers he was initiated into the world of bush flying.

I was enchanted, not just by his stories, but by the wonder and innocence I sensed in the storyteller. He sounded like a young man who had just discovered that all his dreams were possible. In the midst of this wonder and dreaming, I discovered something else: a primer for young and would-be bush pilots, or a nostalgic reminder for those who had already mastered the world of bush flying.

I also discovered in those three tapes a slice of American history. During the two summers Ted received his initiation into bush flying, he was working for the Coast and Geodetic Survey, a forerunner of today's National Oceanic and Atmospheric Administration (NOAA). His work involved flying supplies and personnel for one of the survey teams charged with the first comprehensive mapping of the territory of Alaska. It was an urgent assignment, triggered by the heating up of the Cold War.

I knew that without Ted here to verify and clarify the information it would take a lot of research to make a book out of these tapes, but I was certain there was a book there, one that I was sure would not just entertain, but inspire and inform. I also knew, to make it all work, I would need pictures.

Nancy vaguely remembered that Ted had many old pictures, but still reeling from her loss, she had neither the time nor the heart to search for them. However, she told me that if they existed, they would be somewhere in the basement, and I was welcome to look for them.

The basement was packed from floor to ceiling with furniture, clothing, books. At first glance, the task seemed overwhelming, but I dug in and was eventually rewarded for my efforts. I found two boxes of slides marked the summers of '51 and '52.

Since the pictures were taken nearly fifty years ago, and Ted was not available to identify everyone, at first I hesitated to include them. However, they captured the spirit of Ted's adventure in a way that words alone could not. I felt strongly that they belonged in the book. To that end, I made an effort to obtain whatever identifications I could, seeking out people who, though not connected with the project, might recognize some of the individuals. In some cases I feel confident that I have succeeded. Others have been identified with less confidence, and if I have erred, I apologize. Where I could find no one to identify the individual, I have simply omitted the name.

While looking for pictures of the Coast and Geodetic Survey project, I came across a box of slides marked Stewart, British Columbia, dated four years later—1956. One of the stories Ted had taped for our original book took place in that year and location.

Since I had no plans to do anything with those original stories, I didn't understand why I felt compelled to take these slides, too, but I did. For the next couple years, between assignments, I worked on Ted's book, documenting his experiences in the summers of '51 and '52. It took me another year and a half to find a publisher who was as enchanted with the story as I was. His only regret was that there wasn't more of it.

I mulled this thought over. The book was about Ted's initiation as a bush pilot. Without Ted here, where could I get more information about those two summers he flew for the U.S. Coast and Geodetic Survey? That, after all, is when it all happened. Or did it? Remembering one of the stories from our original book, I realized that his initiation was not really completed until 1956. Not until the summer he worked for a prospector in British Columbia and mastered the dicey maneuver of flying onto and off of a glacier using pontoons.

Suddenly, I understood why I had felt so compelled to take the extra box of slides I found in Ted's basement. Ted was nudging me. He once told me that, for him, the most important story in our original book, the story that inspired him to try to write the book, was the one about that prospector, Tommy McQuillan. Tommy, he said, had been his inspiration and mentor, the man he tried to emulate in his life.

As I was writing *Land Here? You Bet!*, I must admit that I had some concerns about whether Ted would have approved. While he was an outgoing man, he was also a private person. But when I added Ted's experience with Tommy to the book, that concern disappeared because I knew that this new book would now give Ted the chance to accomplish one of his most important goals for our original book—paying proper tribute to his old mentor, Tommy McQuillan. Wherever Ted is now, I am sure he is pleased.

I have chosen to write the book in first person because this is, after all, Ted's story. I want the reader to get a real sense of who he was as a young man. While I have added background information not included in Ted's original tapes, and have on occasion expanded the information he gave me about an incident to provide a fuller picture of what happened, the basic facts are as he recorded them. In expanding on his story, I have gone to other reliable sources—friends, family, historic documentation from the Coast and Geodetic

Survey archives. But, always, I have tried to stay close to the intent and spirit of what Ted told me.

I could never have written this book without the help of many people. Ted, of course, and his wife, Nancy, and Ted's brother, James Huntley, and his wife, Coleen, who encouraged me and provided me with invaluable resources. My thanks also to Ted's cousin, Bob Munro, and his son, Greg, from Kenmore Air Harbor, who provided both information and pictures for the book, and Ted's friends, Bill Peters, Tom Wardleigh, Marsh Terry, and Eric and Tina Barnes. I am also indebted to Captain Skip Theberge, NOAA Corps (ret.) of the NOAA Central Library, who guided me through NOAA's voluminous files on the Coast and Geodetic Survey and helped me find maps and additional pictures from NOAA's archives, and to Rear Admiral Harley Nygren, a former Coast and Geodetic Survey team leader who kindly checked my manuscript for accuracy regarding the organization. I would also like to thank William Ross of Stewart, British Columbia, who generously helped me retrace Ted's flights on and off the Leduc Glacier and throughout the Stewart area. A special thanks goes to my son, Alan Fader, the best editor I have ever worked with, and Rick Emaus and Walt Green, who helped create the map tracing Ted's flight from Seattle to St. Lawrence Island. And, finally, I would like to thank my patient and always encouraging husband, Steve Baker, who provided the security and support that enabled me to finish this book.

A word about the title of this book: Anyone who knew Ted knows that no matter what you ever asked of him, the answer was always the same: Not "I'll try," or "Perhaps," but a firm, confident, "You bet!" As I reviewed his tapes, it became clear that this was the answer he consistently gave the bush pilot and the commander of the C&GS survey team he worked for those two summers in the early '50s, and Tommy McQuillan the summer he flew off glaciers for him in British Columbia. Ted just seemed to "You bet" his way through every challenge he faced, until he earned the right to be called a bush pilot. I can think of no phrase that better reflects the energy and optimism that drove this man throughout his life, or any better title for these early adventures than *Land Here? You Bet!*

— SUNNY FADER

12

Introduction

Setting the Stage

I t's late spring, 1951. Harry Truman is president. James Jones's World War II novel, *From Here to Eternity*, tops the best-sellers list. The big move to the suburbs is on, and families crowd around their television sets every Tuesday night to watch "Uncle Miltie's" antics on the "Texaco Star Theater."

On the sports scene, New York Yankees fans bid farewell to the retiring Joltin' Joe DiMaggio and welcome a rookie named Mickey Mantle to the club. Across town, a twenty-year-old with the New York Giants by the name of William Howard Mays begins the season with a disappointing run of strikeouts before he catches fire and ends up "Rookie of the Year." And because of a turn of events on the world scene, 3,000 miles (4,800 km) away, in Pullman, Washington, another twenty-year-old by the name of Ted Huntley is about to face an unexpected opportunity that will change the course of his life.

In this spring of 1951, the promised peace after World War II has grown uneasy. President Truman has just pronounced Russia "a worldwide aggressor," and the Cold War is official. Defense becomes the country's top priority. With Alaska just thirty-eight miles (61 km) across the Bering Strait from America's new archenemy, the government decides to install a radar defense system there. But there is a problem. The territory is still unmapped. While he doesn't know it yet, this fact is about to present Ted with a chance to fulfill his greatest dream—the dream of becoming an Alaskan bush pilot.

The dream is understandable. The Alaskan bush has been a magnet for adventurers ever since the first Europeans set foot in the area in the early 1800s. What they found was a vast, challenging, breathtakingly beautiful land peopled by Inuits, Athabascans, Tlingits, Haidas and Aleuts, who over the centuries had learned how to survive in this inhospitable terrain. It was the Aleuts who gave Alaska its name; a word thought to mean "mainland" or "land that is not an island," which originally referred to just the Alaskan Peninsula, but eventually came to designate the entire region.

In 1951, statehood was still eight years away, but a small European and American presence had established itself in Alaska and had produced a new hardy, resourceful breed of pilot, the Alaskan bush pilot.

For Ted, himself an aspiring young pilot, these men were heroes. Their legendary feats fired his imagination. He read everything he could find about them, and dreamed of a day when he, too, could test his courage and flying skills in the uncharted bush of Alaska.

In terms of geography and weather, each of Alaska's four regions—the Pacific mountain system of the south, the central region of uplands and lowlands, the Brooks Range (the northernmost extension of the Rocky Mountains) and the Arctic coastal plain, or North Slope—offers its own special challenges to a pilot. Because of a twist of fate, Ted is about to get the chance to experience them all. This summer of 1951 will mark the beginning of his initiation into the world of bush flying, an adventure that, over the next few summers, will take him not only into the Alaskan bush, but into the bush of British Columbia. This is the story of those adventures, as Ted Huntley remembered them.

Chapter 1

The Right Place
at the Right Time

E ver notice how sometimes what seems like the worst piece of
bad luck can turn out to be the best thing that could possibly
happen? That's the way it was for me in the spring of 1951. My
name is Ted Huntley, and I had just completed my second year as a
hotel administration and resort management student at the State
College campus in Pullman, Washington. For the next three months,
I was planning to forget about books and exams and concentrate on
my first love—flying. I piled a semester's accumulation of "stuff"
into my green, restored 1937 Chevy and headed back to Seattle for
what I was sure would be my best summer ever. It was all I had been
thinking about since Easter break.

All through high school and during summer and vacation breaks
from college, I worked at my cousin Bob Munro's seaplane facility,
Kenmore Air Harbor. Bob was only twenty-five when, shortly after
World War II, he and two friends, Reg Collins and Jack Mines,
started Kenmore, but he was well qualified to take on such a venture. After receiving his education in aircraft maintenance at the
Boeing school in Oakland, California, Bob worked as a mechanic
for Pan American World Airways and then as a ground-school
instructor of mechanics.

As soon as I heard Bob was planning to start his flying business,
I decided to ask him for a job. After all, I knew he was going to need
plenty of muscle setting up the air harbor, with all the dredging and
fill work that had to be done on the property. Although I was only

fifteen at the time and, admittedly, a little on the scrawny side, I was already more than six-feet (180-cm) tall and capable, at least in my mind, of doing a man's day's work. My plan was to offer to trade my labor for flying lessons.

I got my opportunity to plead my case during one of Bob's frequent visits to our home in Seahurst, Washington, although, as it turned out, it didn't take much pleading. My cousin Bob comes from hardy Scandinavian-Canadian stock, not a man to waste words or belabor decisions. He looked at me for a moment, then over at my mother. When she did not offer any objections, he said, "Well, yah—yah, you can do that."

Getting the job was easier than I had expected. Getting to work was another story. At fifteen, driving wasn't an option, and Seahurst, where I lived, is at the southern end of Seattle. Kenmore, where Bob had decided to open his new facility, is near Bothell, at the northern end of the city. The bus line was the Suburban Transportation System. I would get to the bus stop at five-thirty in the morning. This would get me to downtown Seattle at quarter to seven, where I would catch another bus for Bothell and get off at Kenmore, arriving at work at quarter after eight—fifteen minutes late. But no one ever complained.

After working all day, I would take the bus home, reaching Seahurst at a little after nine o'clock in the evening. I was paid the minimum wage, which in 1946 was forty cents an hour, so my bus fare consumed the greatest part of my salary. Fortunately, my mother, who saw my working and learning to fly as worthwhile endeavors, helped subsidize my venture.

The Kenmore Air Harbor was built on the site of a shingle mill, on a bog on the north end of Lake Washington. After I turned sixteen, one of my jobs was driving a truck across the highway up above, filling the truck bed with sand from a hillside, and driving back down and dumping the load off where we were constructing a seaplane ramp. Most of this was done in four-wheel drive because the road had been built on top of the shingle shavings, which were bogging down into the marshy ground.

Through Bob's efforts, the Seattle-based company on the shore of Lake Washington became the largest privately owned seaplane base in the world, with a staff today of more than seventy people. But, back in 1951, there was just Bob, his two partners and me. It is a personal point of pride for me to think that I was Kenmore's first employee.

Driving a truck was just one of the things I learned while working weekends during school and full-time in the summer. I also learned how to repair airplanes, pump floats, wipe windshields, clean toilets and, finally, fly.

My love affair with flying, however, began long before Kenmore. I can remember the exact moment I decided I was going to be a pilot. It was in the winter of 1939. I was ten years old and my older brother, Jim, and I were on one of our traditional Sunday afternoon outings with my step-grandfather, Robert C. Levesque, in his 1937 electric-shift Hudson.

My step-grandfather, a quick, friendly French Canadian, used to spend every Sunday, his only day off, creating new adventures for us. This particular day, as frequently happened on these occasions, we ended up at Boeing Field. In those days, you could still drive right up to the field and stroll around the runway. The barnstormers were all lined up, trying to entice anyone with the courage, and five dollars, to take a spin with them. Naturally, I wanted to take them up on their offer, but not my grandfather. "Oh, no, boys! Oh, no," he would say. "We won't do that." Grandfather Levesque believed that it was important to make Jim and me aware of the latest technology. He just didn't trust it.

On this particular day, we had just finished looking at a Stinson Gullwing. The aircraft was sporting a fresh, two-tone green paint job, smartened up with a yellow pinstripe, wheel-pants and chrome-plated push rods. I thought that it was the most beautiful aircraft in the world, until I spotted the DC-3. It was coming in for a landing. I watched, awestruck, as the DC-3 touched down, swung around and came to a stop. As I looked up toward the cockpit, the pilot pulled the window back and smiled at me. It was in that split second that my lifelong love affair with flying was born.

From that day on, no matter where I was or what I was doing, whenever a plane passed overhead, I would stop and look up. Many were Boeing airplanes on experimental flights, including the 314 Flying Boat (a four-engine clipper), the Stratoliner, the B-17, and, during the war years, the Sea Ranger and an experimental fighter with counter-rotating props. I put together a scrapbook about pilots and airplanes for a Cub Scout project. For the next five years, I read everything I could get my hands on about flying and dreamed of the day I would be the one behind the controls. I finally got my chance in the spring of 1946.

Being able to trade my labor for flying time was a tremendous opportunity. As I said, I was paid forty cents an hour. Flying time with an instructor in a sixty-five-horsepower Aeronca Champion cost twelve dollars an hour. That meant if I worked a ten-hour day, I could go flying for twenty minutes with a flight instructor.

I learned the importance of wind, and patience, early in my flying education. My first lesson came the day I took a parachute in for repair and Bob's partner and Kenmore's chief pilot, Jack Mines, agreed to fly me over to Lake Union where I could catch a bus to the service shop. He promised to give me my long-awaited first flying lesson on the way. You can imagine how excited I was.

We taxied out for our takeoff—but we never took off. There was no wind. Without wind, Jack couldn't get the Aeronca up on the step, an angled surface on the underside of a pontoon. With sufficient wind to propel him, a pilot can lift the nose of the plane slightly and, like a motorboat, skim across the surface of the water, gathering enough speed for a takeoff. If there isn't enough wind to get up on the step, the plane cannot take off. Unfortunately, I had to wait another whole week before I finally got that first lesson.

With my flying lessons limited to twenty minutes on weekends and school holidays, it took me a year to get the eight-and-a-half hours of dual instruction I needed to solo. My final instructor, an engineering student at the University of Washington and an Army Air Force veteran, signed me off on a beautiful April day in 1946. I was now free to fly alone and be solely responsible for the aircraft. To celebrate, my "friends" at Kenmore, in keeping with tradition, promptly threw me into Lake Washington.

I continued to trade my labor for flying time until, two years later, at the age of eighteen, I qualified for my commercial pilot's certificate. After that, I was paid to fly! By 1951, I was spending my college breaks working at Kenmore as a mechanic and flight instructor, fixing seaplanes and teaching people to fly. But this summer was going to be different.

In February, my cousin Bob and his partners had launched a new scheduled passenger service out of Kenmore, through the San Juan Islands to Bellingham, Washington. During my spring break in

March, Bob had let me fly the run for a week. It was glorious! Every morning I would climb into the cockpit of the company's Republic Seabee and fly passengers to Friday Harbor and across to Orcas, then on to the other islands. When we reached Bellingham, I would drive downtown, drop off my remaining incoming passengers and pick up any outgoing passengers. Back at the airport, I would load my passengers and take off once again over the San Juan Archipelago, with a turn at Friday Harbor, finally landing back in Seattle. I guess I did a satisfactory job that week because Bob promised me that I could take over from him as pilot for the commuter route when I returned to Kenmore for the summer.

My first morning back in Seattle I showed up for work early, eager to get started. I couldn't wait to get that Republic Seabee in the air. This was, after all, my first true commercial flying job, and with a scheduled airline. (Never mind that it had only one plane.) Bob delivered the bad news as soon as I arrived: the commuter service had been canceled.

"We just didn't get the passengers," he told me, "and we couldn't go on losing money, you understand?"

I understood, but that didn't make me feel any better. The dream I had coveted for the past three months had just gone up in smoke. My disappointment quickly turned into depression. The only antidote I knew for depression was work, so I put on my coveralls and headed for the hangar.

For the next two days, I moved around from one job to the next on automatic pilot, feeling sorry for myself. It's not that I didn't still enjoy working on the planes and teaching people to fly, but it's hard to muster up enthusiasm for an old routine when a promising new adventure has just been snatched from your grasp. Then, on my third day back, something happened that left no more time for self-pity.

Back in April, an Alaskan bush pilot named Nat Brown had contracted with Kenmore to put sixteen brand-new Super Cubs on floats. The first eight had been completed. Brown had already guided them and their pilots to Alaska. Now he was back for the next eight. He needed them in a hurry to fulfill a contract he had with the Coast and Geodetic Survey. My lost opportunity was quickly forgotten as we pulled out all stops to meet the pressing deadline.

Over the years, I had watched an impressive parade of Alaskan

19

bush pilots come through Kenmore. Men like Joe Crosson, who is probably the best known Alaskan bush pilot in the world, a reputation he gained not from his extraordinary record of rescues, but for a single act that moved a bereaved nation. He was the pilot who brought out the bodies of Will Rogers and Wiley Post after their fatal crash in Alaska. And there was Noel Wein, who went from barnstorming to bush flying. He transported everything from gold dust to malamutes in a territory that was still virtually unmapped, and he did it with few instruments, almost no communications and usually without benefit of a runway. He was the first pilot to fly round-trip between America and Asia, and the airline he founded, Wein Airlines, was the first to fly the Arctic route on a scheduled basis. There were also float-flying pioneers like Shell Simmons and Bob Ellis.

For years I had dreamed about following the trails these men had blazed. It was a "some day" kind of dream. That is, until I learned that one of the pilots Nat Brown had hired for his second group of Alaska-bound Cubs had backed out at the last minute.

There I was, with my summer flying job gone. And there was Nat Brown, in desperate need of a pilot, although, admittedly, one with more experience than I had to offer. Looking back, I'm not sure how I found the courage to approach him. He was a gruff man, and his legendary reputation made him seem larger than life. Actually, at six feet and five inches (193 cm) and weighing in at about 275 pounds (124 kg), you might say Nat was larger than life. But my greatest fear—the one that almost stopped me—was that this crusty bear of a man, whom I held in such awe, would find my request laughable. I was, after all, just twenty years old and I had no bush experience. I couldn't bear the thought of having him laugh at me. Still, I knew that an opportunity like this might never come again.

I finally located Nat in the hangar. He was checking out some of the newly installed floats.

"Excuse me, Mr. Brown."

"Yeah, what is it, kid?"

"I understand you're looking for a pilot."

"That's right. You know somebody?"

I took a deep breath and plunged in.

"Well, sir, I have about 500 hours of flying time, 400 of it on water and about 100 on land. And since my job flying here at

Kenmore this summer has sort of gone away, I sure would like to fly for you in Alaska."

For what seemed like an eternity, Nat just stood there, staring at me. Finally, he said, "Well, I'll think about it."

Not for long, I thought to myself as he walked away. I knew he was scheduled to take off for Alaska with his pilots and eight Cubs first thing in the morning. This fact, if nothing else, was in my favor. I watched him disappear into my cousin Bob's office. It was only natural that he would check with him before making his decision. After all, Bob was my boss. Nat didn't know that he was also my first cousin. I wasn't sure, at this point, whether that would turn out to be an advantage or disadvantage.

In hindsight, I realized that I probably should have consulted Bob before approaching Nat. I had just put my cousin in an awkward position, not only professionally, but personally. If Bob recommended me for the job, and something happened to me while flying in Alaska, my mother might never forgive him. On the other hand, if he didn't recommend me, especially after the commuter flying job fell through, he had to be thinking that I would never forgive him. I am not sure whether I would have or not.

There was no use waiting around, worrying about what was going on in Bob's office. It was out of my hands now, so I went back to work. About fifteen minutes later, I felt a tap on my shoulder and turned to find Nat looking down at me.

"Okay, kid, you got it. Can you be ready by tomorrow morning?"

"You bet! What'll I need?"

"A pair of hip boots, a warm leather jacket, a good sleeping bag and about three or four sets of underwear." Later, my cousin Bob suggested that I add a Winchester 32 special rifle, some mosquito netting and a large supply of warm wool socks to the list.

"There's just one other thing, Mr. Brown," I called after him as he started to walk away.

"Nat."

"Nat. I ... I've never flown a Super Cub. Would it be all right if I took one up this afternoon so I'll be ready to fly tomorrow?"

"Yeah, kid," he chuckled. "I think that's a real good idea."

As it happened, the weather to the north turned bad and we didn't leave the next day as scheduled. This gave me a chance to get about three or four hours of takeoffs, landings and slow flight under my belt before we headed for Alaska. The Piper Super Cub had a 135-horsepower Avco Lycoming engine and was on 1400 floats. The float size refers to the weight the floats are designed to carry. If an airplane grosses 1,400 pounds (630 kg), the 1400 floats will sit halfway into the water when the plane is at full gross weight.

Nat's Cubs were actually licensed at 1,500 pounds (675 kg), but in 1951 they weren't making 1500 floats, so he had to settle for slightly undersized floats. During my practice flights, I found the undersized floats to be an advantage. With a light load the plane skipped over the water and virtually leapt into the air. Once I got to Alaska, however, I discovered that the undersized floats made taking off with a full load tricky. The plane tended to bury either its left or right float, depending on the direction of the wind.

The weather delay also gave me a chance to fly up and see my mother before I left for Alaska. At that time, I was staying with Bob, and she was living at a cousin's house at the end of Lake Sammamish, near Issaquah. If she had any misgivings about her twenty-year-old son heading out into the Alaskan wilderness, she never voiced them. Or, perhaps, in my enthusiasm over my unbelievably good luck, I just never heard them. I kissed her on the cheek, assured her that I would take good care of myself, promised to write and headed back to Kenmore to complete my preparations.

On the way back, I gave silent thanks for the cancellation of the commuter route. If my original dream had come true, that obligation would have made flying for Nat Brown impossible ... and I would have missed one of the greatest adventures of my life.

The Cubs, which had been flown to Kenmore directly from the factory in Lockhaven, Pennsylvania, had fewer than thirty hours on the log. They even smelled new. They had big red numbers painted on the side of the fuselage over a small maroon racing stripe that ran from the engine to the tail. The planes themselves were glacier gray, and the floats silver. This color combination, I discovered later, rendered them virtually invisible in the Arctic mist.

On May 15, two days behind schedule, the weather cleared sufficiently for us to take off. We packed our gear into our respective planes and lined up behind Nat's 115-horsepower yellow Super Cub. One by one, we took to the air and headed north.

Chapter 2

Flying to Alaska

By the time we reached the middle of Vancouver Island in Canada, it became apparent that the weather was not going to continue to cooperate for the duration of our trip to Alaska. Nat decided we would spend the night at Sullivan Bay, a protected little harbor at the north end of the island, on the mainland side. There was an old logging camp there that had been converted into a refueling point to service the many seaplanes that traveled up and down the coast of British Columbia. Still playing follow the leader, one by one, we snuck in under the cloud cover and touched down on the mirror-like bay.

Because the cliffs at Sullivan Bay go straight down into the water, we had to tie our planes up to large log floats. The facilities at Sullivan Bay, which included a couple of cabins, a mess hall and a cook's building, were also on log floats. After dinner we all settled in for the night, hoping to get an early start in the morning. Unfortunately, the next day the weather was still poor to the north, toward Ketchikan, our next scheduled refueling spot. We had a good breakfast, tended to our planes and spent the rest of the day reading, walking around and fishing. We caught about ten or twelve small trout just by casting off the floats of our planes.

This unscheduled downtime gave me a chance to meet some of the other pilots working with Nat. Most of them were military veterans of World War II. Some were fighter pilots; two of them were navy pilots who had flown off carriers. One of the civilian pilots had flown transports. The other civilian pilot, John Gallagher, whom I got to know pretty well that summer, was, like me, a mechanic as well as a pilot, but he had about 1,000 flying hours, double my experience. However, John had just recently gotten his seaplane rating. In fact, much to my surprise, it turned out that, while I was the youngest and, in terms of hours, the least experienced pilot in the group, I was the most experienced on the water. That was because, having learned to fly out of Kenmore, seaplanes were all I got to fly for the first 300 hours of my experience. The rest of the pilots had racked up their experience on wheels and had gotten their seaplane rating in less than five hours.

About noon, as we were enjoying a lunch of fresh-caught trout, a DeHavilland Beaver—a brand-new airplane in those days—taxied up. While the plane was being refueled, the Beaver's pilot and his three passengers came into the mess hall for lunch. Unable to contain my curiosity about this new airplane, I struck up a conversation with the pilot.

"I'm telling you, there's nothing in the sky that even comes close to matching it," he boasted. "It's been designed specifically for working the bush. Carries seven or eight people. And it's got a 450-horsepower Pratt and Whitney engine that makes it come right up out of the water and follow the propeller into the air."

Nat's raised eyebrow confirmed that he shared my reservations. That was all I needed.

"I think maybe this new Super Cub can probably perform just as well as that Beaver," I said.

"Not a chance," the Beaver's pilot insisted, pulling a ten spot from his pocket. "I'll put up ten dollars right here and now that says that Cub can't even come close to getting off the water as quick. Not even with just a pilot ... and me and my three passengers in the Beaver."

I looked at Nat. He nodded.

"All right," I said, producing my own ten-dollar bill.

The man who owned the fueling facility agreed to take charge of the money. If the Beaver's pilot won, he could pick up his winnings on his way back down the coast. If I won, I would collect my winnings when I landed.

A small crowd gathered as we taxied out to the starting point, me with a full fuel tank and an empty plane; the Beaver's pilot all fueled up, with his three passengers. Someone on shore waved a red shirt. We began our takeoff. The Beaver's pilot was just coming up on the step when my Cub broke over onto the step and was up in the air in almost one motion, beating the Beaver out of the water by probably 200 feet (60 m). I came back around, landed, collected my winnings and offered them to Nat.

"Nah, kid," he said. "You keep it." I put the money in my pocket. My summer was certainly off to a good start. I hadn't even reached Alaska yet and I was already ten dollars ahead.

We copied the weather reports out of Ketchikan hourly. Two more days passed before there was any indication of reasonable flying weather ahead. When the good news came, we took off immediately.

It is approximately 400 miles (640 km) from Sullivan Bay to Ketchikan. One minute the sun would be out and the air would be calm. The next, visibility would suddenly drop to two miles (3.2 km), and gusty winds and driving rains would pelt the Super Cubs. I had to work continually just to stay in the air. Fortunately, when we finally reached Ketchikan four-and-a-half hours later, we found a light wind and a comfortable 2,000- to 3,000-foot (600- to 900-m) ceiling with sunlight streaming brightly through breaks in the overcast sky.

The seaplane facilities in Ketchikan were right up against the docks on the shoreline, so there wasn't enough room to take in all eight Cubs at the same time. Nat went first, parking his airplane at the Ellis Airlines' float. That left room for one more Super Cub to come in and gas up. Then Nat would push the newly filled Cub off, and the next Super Cub would come in.

This routine left the rest of us bobbing out in the middle of the straits, waiting our turn at the dock, and it left me with a problem. After all those hours of flying, I was in urgent need of a personal pit stop, but there were six Cubs ahead of me. Looking around, I discovered my colleagues had already solved the problem. They were standing on their floats, relieving themselves, right there in the middle of the harbor, in front of God and everybody. Trying not to think about what my mother might say regarding such an immodest display of camaraderie, I quickly joined them.

Juneau, to the north, was still reporting bad weather, so after refueling we headed for Sitka, on Baranof Island. Nat knew bad weather tends to be worse inland, so he took the coastal route, leading us across Chatham Straits. We flew in tight formation, one airplane directly behind the other. Visibility was still poor. At times I could barely make out the tail of the plane in front of me.

As we reached the southern tip of Baranof Island and started up the coast, I could see the huge Pacific storm waves, all the way from Australia, crashing against the shoreline. They exploded against the rocks, spraying our low-flying Cubs. Sometimes, the waves hit with such force that the spray shot above our airplanes.

One cardinal rule my cousin Bob had taught me about flying was to always be aware of my options in case of a sudden loss of power. Looking around, I realized that there was no way I could land on the water and survive. If anything happened, my only chance would be to try to hang it in the trees and hope for the best. It wasn't a very comforting thought.

We finally got a break in the weather about thirty miles (48 km) from Sitka. At last I could relax a little. That's when the fatigue kicked in. Since leaving Sullivan Bay that morning, we had logged—mostly in weather thick as pea soup—more than seven hours of flying time. I was feeling dog tired.

Then I got my first glimpse of Sitka, nestled on the west side of Baranof Island. The view took my breath away and, suddenly, I wasn't tired anymore.

The village is flanked on the east by majestic snow-capped mountains, and on the west by the Pacific Ocean. I had seen pictures and read stories about Alaska's magnificent vistas, but words and pictures can't compare with a firsthand experience. The ornate domes of the nearly century-old Russian Orthodox St. Michael's Cathedral towered over Sitka's magnificent, craggy harbor. For me, at that moment, Sitka had to be the prettiest town in Alaska.

Nat led us into the inner harbor. We tied our airplanes up to a log boom and headed to town for a meal and a good night's sleep.

Sitka is 185 air-miles (296 km) northwest of Ketchikan and ninety-five miles (152 km) southwest of Juneau. It was originally inhabited by a major tribe of Tlingits, who called the village "Shee Atika." In 1799, the Russians arrived. They renamed it Novo Arkhangelsk, or New Archangel, and for seventy years, it was the capital of Russian America.

Then, in 1867, in what I would call one of the shrewdest real-estate deals in U.S. history, the United States took possession of Alaska for $7.2 million and renamed New Archangel Sitka, in deference to its original Tlingit name.

During the mid-1800s, when Los Angeles was just a mission and San Francisco a tent city, Sitka was already a major port, the "Paris of the Pacific." It had a population of 2,000 and boasted an industrial forge, shipwrights, a scientific station and a cathedral. Furs destined for European and Asian markets were its main export, but fish, lumber and ice were also exported to Hawaii, Mexico and California. Gold mines contributed to its growth in the early 1900s. Sitka remained the capital of the territory after the United States took over until 1906, when the seat of government was moved to Juneau.

By 1951, when I made my first visit to Sitka, I found many Tlingits there, and some Haidas, Eskimos and Aleuts, as well as a number of enterprising Americans. The Russians were long gone, but their presence was, and is still felt. They left an indelible mark on the art, architecture and culture of this unique little village.

Because Sitka is located on the very edge of the Pacific Ocean, you won't find as many clouds there as you find farther east, where the maritime air has to make its way between the hills and into the crags of the mountains. This means that you have a better chance of waking up to good weather in the little Russian village than in many other towns in southeastern Alaska. The next morning we awoke to a clear blue sky dotted with bright, puffy cumulus clouds. Perfect flying weather.

The weather held for the first part of the next leg of our journey. Visibility was around fifty miles (80 km) as we once again headed northwest along the coast of Baranof Island, toward Yakutat. The scenery was spectacular. My sightseeing, however, ended abruptly when we reached Cape Spencer at the northern end of the Inside Passage.

From this point on, as Nat led us across the passage entrance and north along the shoreline, where the glaciers come down the mountains, break up and fall into the ocean, the ceiling kept dropping. And so did the Cubs. We were now flying, single file, just a 100, sometimes only fifty feet (30–15 m) above the angry Pacific. Visibility was two to three miles (3.2–4.8 km). I could make out one or two Cubs ahead of me and tried to keep a sharp eye out for the others. When we passed Mt. Fairweather, the rocky shore below gave way to mile after mile of sandy beach. The refueling stop at Yakutat was pretty much a repeat of Ketchikan. We set down in the bay and moved into the beach, two by two. There was one difference. At Yakutat, we had to fill up using five-gallon (23-l) cans. Each plane took approximately twenty-five gallons (113 l). Twenty-five gallons times eight plus Nat's plane is 225 gallons (1,013 l). With our fuel tanks filled, we jumped into the air and continued our journey north.

At one point, I spotted a huge grizzly bear stalking salmon at the edge of the water. The bear's abundant hide created the illusion of a graceful creature gliding along the beach in an oversized fur coat that rippled and flowed around him as he moved. As we flew over him, he turned, rose on his hind legs and swatted at us with his massive paw, as if we were a bunch of pesky, oversized buzzing flies.

Nat continued to lead us north, past the face of the Malaspina Glacier, rising from sea level to its origins on 19,800-foot (5,940-m) Mt. Logan. The Malaspina Glacier is the largest glacier on the North American continent. It is as big as the entire state of Rhode Island.

From my vantage point, I could see giant potholes on the glacier, with huge trees in them. There had been enough gravel and dirt there at one time for the trees to take root. They probably grew on top of the glacier for some 150 to 200 years before they became so large that the ice beneath them collapsed under their weight, sucking the trees into the holes.

Our procession of Cubs flew on, past Cape Yakataga and the Bering Glacier, and past Katalla, where oil was first discovered in Alaska. As we made our way across the Copper River flats, visibility was down again to about two to three miles (3.2–4.8 km). Our next stop was Cordova, on Eyak Lake. When we got there, we found fifteen-mile-an-hour (24-km-an-hour) winds and the waves running at least a couple feet high. There was a long gravel spit sticking out into the lake. Given the size of the waves, there was no way to tie up in front of the gravel bar without being pounded into the beach.

I touched down and watched as Nat taxied around the gravel bar to the protected waters behind it, using a technique known as "plowing." I was familiar with the technique. I had used it many times to taxi on water in high winds. You don't come up on the step, nor do you go very fast, but you apply a lot of engine power so you have a good blast of air over the tail surfaces, and you move with enough speed so the water rudders are effective. If you hold the aileron into the wing so the wind doesn't come up and put the rudder to the airplane, you can get it to go where you want with plenty of power on.

Taking my lead from Nat, I plowed my way around the tip of the spit, tied down next to his Cub and climbed up on the gravel. Nat was standing at the top like a great colossus, arms akimbo, shaking his head as he watched the other pilots try again and again to get their uncooperative planes around the spit. They were all skilled, capable pilots, but even the most competent pilot needs more than five hours of float-flying experience to master plowing. They would either go too fast and break up on the step, or slow down too much and lose rudder control.

After a while, the scene on the lake began looking like an old Keystone Cops routine, with Cubs nearly bumping into each other as they bobbed up and down, out of control in the choppy water. I knew Nat had some reservations about hiring me because of my age and my lack of bush experience, so I was really pleased when, after watching this chaotic scene for a few moments, he turned to me and announced, "Kid, I think you're going to do okay."

Eventually, all of the pilots made it around the spit. When the Cubs were safely parked, Nat herded us into a couple of cabs and we headed for downtown Cordova. It was around three-thirty in the afternoon. We had been in the air, or on the water, for roughly nine hours, with nothing to eat since early that morning. I, for one, was starved. At the restaurant, as I wolfed down a large bowl of steaming clam chowder, my thoughts drifted ahead to a hot shower and a nice, comfortable, clean bed. I assumed we would be spending the night in Cordova. Nat, however, had other ideas.

"Finish up boys," he announced. "We've got to get back and on to Anchorage."

I wasn't the only one who assumed we were done flying for the day. "Anchorage?" we echoed in unison. Ignoring our reaction, Nat pushed back his chair and headed for the door.

"We've still got to get across Prince William Sound and there's no telling about the weather up ahead, so we'd better get going."

Without further discussion, we all climbed back into our cabs and headed for Eyak Lake. The wind, which was a disadvantage in landing, was an asset on takeoff. Even with full fuel tanks, my Cub leapt into the air in less than 150 feet (45 m). Once airborne, we again formed our single line behind Nat and headed toward Anchorage.

My respect for Nat Brown's navigational skills increased with every mile. Even with our limited visibility, he was able to keep his bearings as we flew north and west between the hundreds of little islands that lay in our path.

Somewhere near Whittier I noticed that one of the Cubs had dropped out of formation and was flying about 300 yards (273 m) off the left wing. I didn't think much about it at the time, not until we reached the pass between Whittier and Turnagain Arm. The snow-covered pass is only 600 feet (180 m) above sea level, but it rises up above the timberline. I knew that in weather like this, it could be as treacherous as any 6,000-foot (1,800-m) pass in my home state of Washington. As a grim reminder of this fact, I could make out below the clear outline of a fuselage from a large wrecked helicopter and, spewed about the ground, the remains of two small planes.

When Nat got close to the pass he decided that it didn't look good enough to go over and turned back to land at Whittier. However, as he began his turn, he looked back and saw the Cub that had strayed out of formation coming right at him. There was no way to pass it on the right—the valley was too narrow. If he tried to pass it on the left, he would fly smack into the formation. So he aborted his turn and flew through the pass, directly into the throat of that lousy weather.

As I followed Nat and the others through the pass, I saw Nat's Cub suddenly drop about 300 feet (90 m). A warning went off in my brain: downdraft ahead! The drop put Nat about 200 feet (60 m) above the ground. He quickly veered off out over Portage Lake.

The next Cub hit the same downdraft, dropped 300 feet (90 m) and followed Nat out over the lake. And the next and the next, each one remaining in formation. Finally, it was my turn. I added full throttle and tried to keep my altitude. But, like everyone else, when I hit the downdraft, I dropped the 300 feet (90 m), leaving my stomach somewhere up in the clouds. All eight Cubs made it around the corner and over Portage Lake where, thankfully, we were rewarded with improved weather that lasted the entire forty-five-mile (72-km) trip through the mountains and over the fjord to Anchorage. In fact, to my amazement, it had actually turned into a beautiful evening.

It was now about seven-thirty in the evening, local time, and still daylight. As we flew down Turnagain Arm, I could see over to the right the tracks of a railroad running alongside a new, nearly completed gravel highway. The highway work crews were still at their labors, rushing to complete the link between Anchorage and Kenai.

I twisted and stretched in my seat, trying to rub a cramp out of my left leg, wondering if the other pilots were as bone-weary as I was. Finally, we reached Lake Hood and Lake Spenard, the two lakes that provide seaplane access to Anchorage. That summer, as they do every summer, hundreds of seaplanes descended on Anchorage, bringing in sightseers, fishermen, researchers, prospectors, adventurers, hunters. Every year, this seasonal influx produces the largest gathering of seaplanes in the world, with Lake Hood alone averaging 800 takeoffs and landings a day. That evening, the shores of both lakes were packed tight with seaplanes. I had never seen so many seaplanes in one place. It was a thrilling sight. We flew between the two lakes and headed for the refueling facility on Lake Hood.

After I finished gassing up my Cub, I joined the other pilots on the dock. We had barely been able to drag ourselves from our airplanes when we first landed, but now everyone appeared rejuvenated.

"You'll love Anchorage, kid," one of the pilots assured me. It turned out that I was the only one in the group who had never been there before. They were all eager to initiate me into the wiles and ways of what, in the early fifties, was still a wide-open frontier town. There was one place they seemed particularly anxious for me to visit: the Green Lantern Restaurant.

"Kid," one of the pilots said, placing a brotherly arm around my shoulder, "you just haven't been to Anchorage until you've been to the Green Lantern."

Perhaps if my stomach hadn't been rumbling so loudly and my mind hadn't been preoccupied with thoughts of food, I might have caught the prurient tone of the comment, or paid more attention to the exaggerated grins it triggered. However, it wasn't until several months later, on another trip, that I discovered that the Green Lantern owed its fame, or perhaps I should say its infamy, not to its food, but to its ability to satisfy another basic appetite. That's when I discovered that the Green Lantern, affectionately known as "the

Green Latrine" by those who frequented it, was actually one of the best-known whorehouses in Alaska. But, my education had to wait because we never did make it into Anchorage that night. Before we had a chance to collect our gear, Nat looked out across Cook Inlet. "You know, you don't see that very often from Anchorage," he said, nodding toward Mt. Susitna. The famous "sleeping lady" looked regal against a backdrop of crisp, clear, blue sky. "I think we'd better go on."

This time Nat's words drew one mighty, unified groan. We had already flown roughly 800 miles (1,280 km) that day. Nat was unmoved. Since he was the boss, we all reluctantly got back into our airplanes and headed northwest for the Kuskokwim River on the other side of the Alaska Range.

As we flew by Mt. Susitna, off to the right I could see Mt. McKinley, at 20,320 feet (6,096 m), the highest point in North America, and Mt. Foraker, more than 13,000-feet (3,900-m) high. The mountains we were heading through were not much smaller. The Alaska Range was formed by some ancient cataclysmic upthrust of the earth's crust. Now, masked under a hoary cloak of ice and snow, it separates Alaska's interior tundra prairie from the Pacific coastal region of the state. This northwestward continuation of the Coast Range mountains and the Rocky Mountains of Canada creates a 600-mile (960-km) arc that stretches from the Aleutian Range in south-central Alaska to the Yukon boundary in southern Alaska.

Like windblown specks, our Cubs rode the air currents between the towering mountains. I paid little attention to the white majesty unfolding below me, glistening in the light of the never-setting summer sun. I was too tired. Besides, the scenery looked familiar. It looked much like Washington's Cascade Mountains, over which I had flown many times. But when I finally reached the Kuskokwim River on the other side of Rainey Pass, I discovered a whole new world.

The Kuskokwim River, which drains into the Bering Sea, meanders though forests of spiky spruce and birch trees, which color the tundra in a hundred shades of green. The sight of it deepened my love affair with Alaska, but failed to take my mind off my stomach. All I had had to eat when we touched down in Cordova was a bowl of chowder, and that was over nine-and-a-half hours ago. What I needed was a good hot meal. A little sleep wouldn't have hurt, either.

As we flew over the river, we passed a little airport on the side of a hill, with a big log cabin at the end of it. Parked on the river in front of the cabin was a Super Cub, just like the ones we were flying. Nat tipped his wings, signaling us to land. Setting down on the Kuskokwim proved to be one more challenge. There was a brisk three- or four-mile-an-hour (4.8- or 6.4-km-an-hour) current on the river. The trick was to get your airplane up on the beach and tied down before the current carried it down river. Once again, my seaplane experience paid off. I made it on the first try and, strongly motivated by my rumbling stomach, hurried to help the others. Surely, I thought, Nat would stay here long enough to let us eat.

The place was called the Cripple Creek Roadhouse, although there was no road around for hundreds of miles. In the Alaska of the early fifties, roadhouses were stopping places for dog-team drivers, people coming up and down the river in their boats and, of course, pilots. I could smell the salmon cooking even before we reached the front door.

Fresh from its watery Arctic home, and grilled to perfection, the salmon we ate that evening was, without a doubt, the best I have ever tasted. I lingered appreciatively over my meal, savoring every mouthful. Nat practically inhaled his dinner and excused himself from the table, explaining that the Cub we had seen parked in front belonged to the first group of eight he had brought to Alaska. It had flipped over a couple days earlier and he needed to make sure that it was still serviceable. Fortunately, the only damage was to its propeller, and a new one had already been ordered. Unfortunately, his inquiry didn't take long. He returned to the dining room just in time to stop us from turning in for the night.

"Tell you what," he bellowed in a cheerful baritone, "it's only two hours more down to Bethel. There's a real good roadhouse down there where we can spend the night."

Even with a good meal under our belts, the thought of climbing back into our planes for another two hours of flying was not exactly welcome; however, from the set of Nat's jaw, it was clear to me that his "suggestion" wasn't up for discussion. One of the other pilots must have missed the signal, because he rose to protest, but Nat quickly cut him off. "We need to get to Bethel tonight," he announced firmly. "We're behind schedule."

By the time we took off, the sun was coming back up—not that it had ever gone down all the way, but just to below the horizon. There is no real darkness during Alaska's nightless summer months, only a kind of twilight for a few hours. In the part of Russia that hugs the Arctic region, the phenomenon is called "white nights." As I got off the water and flew down the Kuskokwim River to the northwest, I felt like the rising sun was burning a hole right through my eyes to the back of my head. Any moment I expected smoke to begin coming out of my ears.

We were now flying over tundra country, filled with potholes and slow streams running through high grass. Even from the air, I could tell that the ground was very wet. It would probably be impossible to walk through by midsummer. In the winter you would need a dog team, and even then you would most likely have to stick to the frozen rivers.

About two hours later, we arrived at Nat's "real good" roadhouse, a godforsaken-looking cabin with an airport, across the river from Bethel. By the way Nat flew into the place, I suspected that he was very familiar with the spot. I found out later that he spent about a third of his flying time in Alaska flying out of Bethel. It was his home away from home.

Now, in 1951, Bethel was not one of Alaska's more scenic spots. The river was silty and brown. In the water along the bank, there was all kinds of junk, including discarded cars and refrigerators. An old Waco biplane, sitting on some kind of a raft, caught my eye as I touched down. The fabric was all pushed through and hanging. It looked like just another piece of junk. It turned out that the Waco belonged to Nat. He, in fact, had planes all over the country; all kinds of planes, from new Cubs like the ones we were flying, to old junkers like that Waco.

The sun grew brighter and brighter as the other pilots and I stumbled toward the roadhouse. I was positive that I'd be asleep the minute my head hit the pillow. It didn't happen. I tossed and turned for what seemed like an eternity, the whine of my engine still pulsing in my ears. My eyebrows and eyeballs burned as if they were on fire. I had been awake for twenty-two-and-a-half hours, thirteen and a half of which I had spent flying. Never in my career, before or since, can I remember a longer day.

Chapter 3

A Change of Plans

When it came time to hand out flying assignments to his pilots, Nat decided to team me up with John Gallagher. I guess he thought that John's considerable experience would compensate for my lack thereof. John and I were scheduled to replace two pilots Nat had working for the U.S. Coast and Geodetic Survey out of the village of Kipnuk, but when the three of us arrived at the village the next day, mutiny was afoot. The two pilots to be replaced refused to leave. It was a simple matter of money.

Nat paid his pilots 800 dollars a month for eighty hours of flying, plus ten dollars for every hour they flew over the eighty. So far that month, the two pilots at Kipnuk had put in 110 hours each, and there were still eight days left in the month. They figured if they stayed until the end of the month, they could squeeze in at least another fifteen or twenty hours of golden time. By 1951 standards, that added up to some pretty impressive money.

Naturally, Nat didn't like that idea. The money was going to have to come out of his profits. He and the pilots started going at it hot and heavy, so I decided to check out the village, not that there was much to see in Kipnuk: a few houses, a school, a Moravian church and a village store. As I came out of the store, Nat motioned to me. The argument was over. The men would stay, and Nat would take John and me on to St. Lawrence Island, somewhere out in the Bering Sea about a 110 miles (176 km) south of Nome, and roughly a 125 miles (200 km) west of the mouth of the Yukon River.

I knew from the knit of his brow that Nat wasn't happy with the arrangement. It wasn't just the money. Kipnuk was a routine flying assignment, something I'm sure Nat felt I could handle. St. Lawrence Island, on the other hand, was a complex and far more challenging assignment. John had the credentials for the job, but I'm certain Nat would rather have had a more experienced pilot for the second slot. Not some twenty-year-old kid he had picked up at the last minute out of desperation. Unfortunately, his schedule and commitments left him no choice. The three of us headed for St. Lawrence Island, by way of Alakanuk, a little village at the mouth of the Yukon River.

Nat led us north out of the Kuskokwim River system, across the flats, toward the mouth of the Yukon. The ceiling was roughly 2,000 feet (600 m), with a little sunlight showing through here and there, but mostly thick dark clouds. We cruised along in single formation, about fifty feet (15 m) under the clouds.

Since John and I were scheduled to work out of Kipnuk, neither of us had brought charts along for this trip. We were totally dependent on Nat to get us to St. Lawrence Island, which is why I became somewhat anxious when I noticed Nat's Cub moving closer and closer to those clouds. Then, about twenty minutes into the flight, Nat's little yellow Cub just drifted up and disappeared into the cloud cover. There was no way we could follow him, not without risking bumping into him. The plan was for us to touch down and refuel in Alakanuk, but without Nat, all we had to guide us there was a general bearing on our whiskey compass, a little compass card that floats in alcohol inside an instrument casing. I hoped ours were pointing in the right direction.

I kept waiting for Nat to drop back down. He didn't. Finally, I spotted a fairly large hole in the clouds. John and I had no radios, so I wiggled my wings to signal him to follow me, and we headed up through the hole. We traveled some 2,500 feet (750 m) through the thick clouds before we broke through the top to beautiful, crystal-clear sunshine—but no sign of Nat.

Guided by our compasses, John and I continued above the clouds for about twenty to twenty-five minutes, all the while keeping a sharp eye out for Nat's yellow Cub. I couldn't believe that my employer would just take off and leave us. We did have one thing going for us in case Nat didn't show up: the Yukon is three- or four-miles (4.8- or 6.4-km) wide at its mouth. Providing our compasses were accurate and guided us into the general location, the river should be easy to spot. However, we would need to be below the clouds to do that. John must have had the same thought. At the next hole, we wiggled our wings at each other and headed back down through the clouds.

We flew along for another twenty or twenty-five minutes. I had just about resigned myself to the idea that John and I were on our own when Nat's Cub dropped down out of the clouds in front of us. Since we hadn't seen him above the clouds, he must have been flying blind right in the midst of them for at least forty minutes. No easy feat with only a whiskey compass to guide you. John and I fell into formation behind Nat and followed him into Alakanuk.

Alakanuk is located about fifteen miles (24 km) from the Bering Sea, at the eastern entrance of Alakanuk Pass, the major southern channel of the Yukon River. It's the longest village on the lower Yukon, covering a three-mile (4.8-km) area along the pass. The village takes its name from the Yupik word "Alarneq," which means "wrong way" or "mistaken village." It supposedly got that name because native fishermen and hunters looking for a summer camp called "Kwiggarpak" would often mistakenly take the Alarneq slough and miss the camp, ending up in Alakanuk instead. Flying in and looking down on the area's maze of waterways, it was easy to see how this could happen.

This was May, and the ice on the river from the freeze-up that began in November was just beginning to break up, but the weather in Alakanuk was still pretty bad. I knew Nat was concerned about being behind schedule and anxious to get John and me to St. Lawrence Island as soon as possible, but the rest of our trip would be over open sea, out of sight of land. Not something an experienced bush pilot like Nat would risk in bad weather. It was decided that we would spend the night in Alakanuk. As it turned out, we ended up spending a couple of days in the little Eskimo village before the weather ahead cleared enough for us to take off again.

Alakanuk was a small Yupik village with a population in the summer of about 200 (around 50 in the winter). Subsistence fishing and hunting were the main means of survival, but some of the Eskimos also worked at the local salmon cannery run by Jack Emel and his family. I had a chance to spend some time with the family and came away quite impressed with its profitable little operation, and with Jack Emel, who during the dark winter months fed his mind by reading history and philosophy, which he would then discuss with the village's resident Jesuit priest.

Life in Alakanuk was pretty basic. The village had no hotel or restaurant. Nat struck up a deal for our food and lodgings with the local postmaster, a lanky old Swede who had come to the Yukon back in the gold rush days, somewhere around 1908. He had done some prospecting around Marshall, Alaska, and eventually settled down with an Eskimo woman with whom he had a son. The old man's wife was long dead and he and his son, now a towering young man half a head taller than his six-foot (180-cm) father, were living a bachelor's life.

Of course, calling what the Swede offered us "food and lodgings" is stretching it a bit. The lodgings turned out to be a room on top of the post office where Nat, John and I found a few cots to stretch our sleeping bags out on. As for the food, the Swede showed us a piece of dried herring, which looked suspiciously like it had been sitting out on the long plank table for some days, and told us to help ourselves.

There wasn't much to do in Alakanuk while we waited out the weather. To bide my time, I took to hanging around the post office, one of the more active spots in the village. One afternoon, a young Eskimo couple came in looking for the Swede. They had a problem, and I got my first lesson in premarital counseling, bush style.

Back when missionaries first started coming to what is now Alaska, each missionary group staked out its own villages. One village might become Moravian, another Lutheran. The Catholics got to Alakanuk first. Every two months or so, a priest would fly in for two or three days on a scheduled bush plane that Northern Consolidated Airlines ran between Alakanuk and Bethel. The priest would hold a few services and take care of all the necessary rituals like funerals, weddings and baptisms, then move on to the next Catholic village— a sort of traveling salesman for God. However, the circuit priest's schedule and the villagers' needs were not always in sync.

"Swede, we want to get married," I heard the young Eskimo man say, in a kind of pidgin English.

The Swede looked down at the couple. "The priest was here last week. Why didn't you do it then?" he asked in his Swedish accent.

"We just decided yesterday."

"Well," the Swede said, "the priest won't be back for another two months."

"We know that, Swede. What should we do?"

The Swede had a single, reddish-gray hair on the top of his head, which he tended to scratch when he was thinking. He scratched it now.

"I'll tell you what," he said finally. "You just go ahead and act like you're married, and the priest will square it away when he gets back."

I started to laugh, but I seemed to be the only one who found the Swede's counsel funny. The young Eskimo couple gravely nodded to each other, then to the Swede, and hand in hand headed for the door to, I suspect, put the sage advice to immediate use.

I went looking for John and Nat. Until now, I had been a prime audience for all the other pilots' Alaskan stories. Now I finally had one of my own to share.

The weather finally cleared enough for us to continue our journey. We took off from Alakanuk, over the ice floe–crowded mouth of the Yukon, and headed out over the Bering Sea. There were ice floes scattered as far as you could see. I hoped that Nat had gotten all his cloud-flying out of his system, because with nothing between us and St. Lawrence Island for the next 125 miles (200 km) but that cold, ice-filled gray sea, I wanted Nat's little yellow Cub right out there in front of me where I could see it.

There wasn't much wind. Nat anticipated that it would take us about an hour and twenty minutes to get to our next landfall, Northeast Cape, the point on St. Lawrence Island closest to the mouth of the Yukon. I thought about that. With all my seaplane experience, I had never flown out of the sight of land for such a long period of time. And there would be no reassuring radio signals out here to guide me. The only way to get where we were going was to fly due west on a compass heading.

We began flying at about 2,000 feet (600 m), but to keep under the clouds we had to let down, then let down again, to about 500 or 600 feet (150–180 m). Visibility was three or four miles (4.8–6.4 km). According to Nat, that was pretty good weather for the Bering Sea. Looking down, I could see that at least the sea wasn't very rough. I could land on it if I had to. But, seeing how far we were from land, the question was, if I did, what then?

After about an hour and thirty minutes, Nat turned slightly to the left, and I spotted a bunch of walruses sliding off what looked to me like a big ice pan, or possibly an island. I wasn't sure. Then I saw more ice and some dark shapes ahead. The shapes turned out to be the bottom 300 feet (90 m) of Northeast Cape. We had reached St. Lawrence Island in just about ten minutes over Nat's predicted time.

St. Lawrence Island is quite large, about 100-miles (160-km) long and twenty-miles (32-km) wide. It has two small Eskimo villages: Gambell and Savoonga. John and I were headed for Gambell, tucked away in the northwest corner of the island.

As prearranged, Nat wiggled his wings to say goodbye, turned north and headed back out over the Bering Sea for Nome, about eighty degrees off to the right. John and I headed west along the coastline for another 120 miles (192 km), keeping the land on our left and the ice pans on our right. Our total flying time that day from Alakanuk to our destination was three hours.

Gambell sits on a gravel deposit at the base of an 800-foot (240-m) cliff, but all I could see of the cliff when we circled the town to land was the bottom 300 feet (90 m). On the gravel below I spotted a group of white and orange houses, obviously government built. I could also see some wooden Eskimo dwellings, a general store and a little pond or lake that was half frozen over. John and I peeled off toward the lake and landed in the water, then taxied up on the edge of the ice, continuing part way into town.

When we shut down our engines, we were greeted by a friendly welcoming committee of Eskimo men. With their help, we tied fifty-gallon (225-l) drums of fuel under the wings of our Cubs, to hold the planes down in the event of strong winds. We also made sure that the backs of the floats were held up solidly, to give the airplanes a negative angle of attack. This way the wind would not be able to get under the wings and lift them.

There are two kinds of Eskimos living in Alaska: the Inuits, who can also be found in Canada and Greenland, and the Yupiks, native to Siberia. The Eskimos in Gambell were Yupiks. Curiously, the Yupik dialect they spoke could barely be understood by Yupiks in other areas of Alaska, but was readily understood by Siberian Yupiks. However, when you think about it, this makes sense. The village of Gambell is roughly 200 miles (320 km) by boat, over the treacherous Bering Sea, from Nome and the Alaskan mainland, but it is only thirty-six miles (58 km) from the Chukotsk Peninsula of Siberia. Therefore, over the years, it would have been far easier for them to maintain contact with the Siberian Yupiks than with Alaska's mainland Yupiks.

Our Cubs secure, John and I slung our gear over our shoulders and walked down into town, no easy task given the texture of the ground. Walking over that beach gravel was like trying to walk over giant marbles set into a spongy mud. You felt like you were sliding and sinking all at the same time. As soon as we reached the village, following the suggestion of our welcoming committee, we went in search of the local schoolteacher.

As was frequently the case in outlying villages like Gambell, the local schoolteacher served as a sort of administrator for the community. When we finally located him at the general store, he promptly went off to check with the weather station about some housing for us. During World War II, Gambell had been home to a weather observation facility with a detachment of some twenty or thirty men and women who lived in the government houses I had seen on my approach. When the war ended, only two families remained to man the post. This left the base with a number of empty houses.

While we waited for the teacher to return, John and I wandered around the general store. Since Gambell's economy was largely based on subsistence harvests from the sea—seal, walrus, fish, and bowhead and gray whales—it isn't surprising that most of the store's merchandise was related to hunting and fishing. I was amazed at the remarkable variety of ammunition, something for every sporting and nonmilitary rifle imaginable. There were huge harpoon-firing rifles, which the villagers used for hunting whales, and sophisticated harpoon tips with an explosive device that triggered them to spread out like an umbrella on penetration. In today's climate of concern for these great leviathans of the sea, this may seem cruel, but you have to remember that, in 1951, the very survival of the people of this village depended on the success of their hunts.

As the schoolteacher had predicted, the people at the weather station were happy to let John and me use one of their empty houses until our client, the Coast and Geodetic Survey, showed up.

If you've never heard of the Coast and Geodetic Survey, it is probably because it no longer exists. Its work is now carried on by various departments of the National Oceanic and Atmospheric Administration (NOAA). But before NOAA was created, the Coast and Geodetic Survey played a critical role in the development of the United States. As its name implies, it was the governmental department that made geodetic control surveys.

Most people are familiar with plane surveying, which is used for such things as local property measuring and general engineering activities. But when a large expanse of land or water has to be charted or mapped, or a major engineering project such as a highway or railroad is planned, geodetic surveying is used. In geodetic surveying, control points and the size, shape and curvature of the earth all play a part in the surveyor's calculations. Without the use of these geodetic controls, the surveyors working in Alaska that summer would not have been able to bring all their individual surveys together to provide an accurate picture of the whole territory.

In 1951, when I first came into contact with the Coast and Geodetic Survey, it was the smallest of the United States seven uniformed branches of service (the army, navy, air force, coast guard, marines and public health service being the other six.) It had about 200 commissioned officers and federal civilian workers, no enlisted personnel, and eight active ships manned by civilian crews. And it had been around almost as long as the United States itself.

The Coast and Geodetic Survey's lineage can be traced back to 1807, when President Thomas Jefferson signed a bill creating the "Survey of the Coast." This was during a time when our nation was concentrated along the Atlantic coastal plane. During the period before the Civil War, the Coast and Geodetic Survey was made up of civilians who worked hand-in-hand with army and naval officers. It was, by the way, the first federal agency to hire female professionals. The agency's men and women charted all our waterways, produced topographic maps of our shorelines and made our marine highways among the best charted in the world.

As our national boundaries moved southward and westward, and eventually into Alaska, so did the engineers and scientists of the Coast and Geodetic Survey, establishing more than one million geodetic survey points, producing close to 1,000 nautical charts and more than 10,000 aeronautical charts.

Whenever the United States went to war, so did the men and women of the Coast and Geodetic Survey. Beginning with the Civil

War, they provided all United States' armed services, wherever in the world they were fighting, with technical expertise. Much of the work was done at the front, with Coast and Geodetic Survey officers subjected to all the hazards incumbent in fighting a war. During World War II, for example, the survey officers served as artillery surveyors, hydrographers, amphibious engineers, beach masters, reconnaissance surveyors for the worldwide aeronautical charting effort, and instructors at service schools. They helped speed up the movement of men and materiel and were instrumental in improving the efficiency of putting ordnance on target. Their skills in developing new instrumentation and methods are credited with saving countless American and Allied lives.

All commercial pilots, in fact anyone who flies in a commercial airline today, owes thanks to these men and women. Their pioneering efforts during World War II, in partnership with the air force, provided us with many of today's civil air routes. In the field of scientific research, the Coast and Geodetic Survey was instrumental in the creation of organizations in geophysical observations and data processing, and the formation of the American Association for the Advancement of Science, the National Academy of Sciences, the American Geophysical Union, and the American Society of Photogrammetry and Remote Sensing.

But back to 1951. John and I had orders to contact Commander John C. Ellerbe, who was scheduled to arrive in Gambell on the Coast and Geodetic Survey's ship, the *Pathfinder*, which, we learned when we reached the village, had been delayed in Nome by bad weather. Although sparsely furnished, the weather station house was clean and proved to be a warm, pleasant place to wait.

The delay gave me a chance to explore the village. Except for our brief stay in Alakanuk, I had never spent any time in an Eskimo village before. I was filled with curiosity. Coming from a place like Seattle, it was difficult for me to understand how these people not only survived, but apparently seemed to thrive in this isolated, desolate, frozen area of the world, living off of what they could harvest from the sea. The citizens of Gambell graciously welcomed John and me into their homes and generously answered my countless questions about their way of life.

My curiosity was especially piqued by the village's umiaks. I was familiar with kayaks—Seattle has many kayak enthusiasts—

but I had never seen an umiak before. Umiaks are walrus-hide-covered hunting boats with driftwood ribs held together by thongs. The schoolteacher had helped the villagers modernize their umiaks by devising a way to add an outboard motor. They couldn't put the motor in the normal location, the stern of their boats, because it would get swamped by waves coming in from the rear. Instead, they made a well, a wooden, box-like structure, about one third of the way up along the keel line, off slightly to one side and high enough so that it was above the water line. They lined the well with folded-over walrus-hide so it wouldn't leak. And that's where they put their twenty-horsepower outboard motor. It worked beautifully.

There was a certain serendipity involved in the way the Eskimos in Gambell approached hunting. They didn't go out in search of game. They waited for the game to come to them. Whenever someone spotted a whale blow or a pan of ice with walruses going by, the men in the village would grab their hunting gear, climb into their umiaks and head out after their quarry.

On our second day in Gambell, a hunting expedition brought in four walruses. The women quickly went to work on the catch. Hide, bone, blubber, organs—everything had a use, even the intestines. I was struck by the enormity of this particular organ. When the women finished stretching them out on the beach, each one must have measured more than 100-feet (30-m) long, and about two- or three-feet (.6- or .9-m) wide. I watched, fascinated, as a dark, round Eskimo woman, knife in hand, moved to the end of one of the protracted intestines and, bending over, quickly traveled the 100 feet (30 m) or more, deftly splitting the organ right up the center as she went. She never straightened up until her task was done.

After the women had cleaned and dried out the intestines, they cut them up and sewed them into raincoats. The finished product was a little smelly, but I was determined to have one. My purchase proved to be the most effective, foul-weather gear I have ever owned. To this day, I regret that I didn't hold on to it after that summer, but at the time I didn't think the smell would go over well back home in Seattle.

Gambell turned out to be a virtual living museum of whaling history. Back in the late 1860s and early 1870s—the heyday of whaling—the Bering Sea and the Arctic Ocean, with their abundance of these great mammals, became a prime hunting ground for

New England's whalers. The ships would often stop off in Gambell to pick up extra crew. Since the Eskimos had little use for money, the captains usually paid them off with equipment. That was how the village acquired its collection of nearly century-old wooden whaling boats. In mainland United States, these relics would have been relegated to a museum, but not in Gambell. In spite of enduring nearly 100 Arctic winters, the meticulously maintained boats were still seaworthy and in constant use. This shouldn't have surprised me. On a remote Arctic island like St. Lawrence, where nature conspires daily to prevent human habitation, survival depends on the population's ability to make maximum use of every possible resource.

High technology had also found its way to Gambell. On the bluff above town, about a mile hike straight up, the air force had set up a temporary radar station. A permanent facility would eventually be built at Northeast Cape, on the other end of the island. Determining the exact location for that proposed facility was one of the jobs scheduled for the Coast and Geodetic Survey team for whom John and I would be flying. In the meantime, the radar equipment was being operated out of a small building on top of the bluff, and the unit's detachment of forty men was encamped on the gravel below.

By our third day in Gambell, John and I had exhausted all the sightseeing possibilities. We were sitting in our borrowed house, trying to fight off boredom, when a messenger arrived from the radar camp. The lieutenant in charge wanted to know if John and I would care to join him and his men for dinner and a screening of a first-run motion picture that had just been flown in. The air force encampment wasn't far—just about a mile and a half (2.4 km) from where John and I were staying—but there was no road, just slick, jagged rocks. Negotiating that slippery mile and a half (2.4 km) without losing our footing proved to be a real challenge. However, we did manage to navigate the distance without any serious damage to our persons.

Dinner was steak, but that wasn't the only gastronomic "treat" we found waiting for us at the radar base. It was there that I had my first sampling of the vitamin-rich delicacy that is the mainstay of the Eskimo diet, muktuk, more commonly known as whale blubber. I found the taste and texture, well, shall we say, interesting? However, I have never had any desire to repeat the experience.

Over dinner, John and I learned about a tragedy that had befallen the unit earlier that spring. One of the camp's enlisted men had set out to relieve the duty sergeant at the radar shack, some 800 feet (240 m) above the camp. The young man never reached the shack. On his way there he ran into a sudden spring snowstorm, not uncommon in the region. They found his body a week and a half later; he had frozen to death.

The next day I discussed the story of the lost airman with some of the villagers I had befriended. They told me that such a tragedy would be unlikely among their people. The airman didn't understand the fickleness of the area's weather. Because the weather was clear when he set out, he was only wearing his basic air force issue. A St. Lawrence Island Eskimo would never make that mistake. He or she would never go anywhere, *any* time of year, regardless of the weather, without their parka, reindeer or caribou pants, warm mitts and a pair of mukluks. Mukluks were handmade, fur-lined, waterproof boots. The fur came from a herd of local reindeer, which had been brought to St. Lawrence Island back in 1939, as part of a project to transplant reindeer herds from Lapland into Alaska.

But there is more to the Eskimos' ability to survive than wearing the right clothes. The Eskimos of St. Lawrence Island lived according to a whole tradition of survival wisdom, learned by every child at his or her mother's knee. For example, they told me that if one of their people got caught in a sudden snowstorm, he (or she) wouldn't waste energy trying to find shelter. He would dig out a little area, lie down in his parka, warm pants and mukluks, and fluff the snow up all around him. Then he would rest in that little burrow until the storm was over, whether that took a few hours, a day or a week. I appreciated the information and filed it away in the back of my mind, hoping, of course, that I would never have a need to use it.

The Cold War, which was just gearing up in the early fifties, had already made an impact on life in Gambell. Many of the Eskimos had family across the Bering Strait, in Russian Siberia. A couple of times a year, the islanders would hop into their umiaks and brave the icy waters to visit their Siberian relatives. But no longer, they told me. About six years earlier, at the end of World War II, they had gone to Siberia, only to be greeted on their arrival by Russian soldiers, who promptly locked them up. The soldiers kept the villagers locked up for almost two weeks before sending them home with a warning never to return. The clampdown was probably prompted by the Russian airbase, across the strait. When the wind was blowing in the right direction, I could hear the Russians' jet engines being run up and the airplanes in the air, just across the international date line, twelve miles (19 km) from where we were.

The emerging Cold War was one of the reasons John and I were on St. Lawrence Island. Along with its regular mapping activities, the Coast and Geodetic Survey team was also determining locations for the building of the DEW (Distant Early Warning Radar System) line sites and White Alice sites the United States was busy setting up throughout the region. The White Alice sites were communication stations that transmitted the information gathered by the radar system. They did this by bouncing waves off the tropopause (a transition zone between the troposphere and the stratosphere) to locations some 150 to 300 miles (240–480 km) from the transmitter. Back in the fifties, this was state-of-the-art technology, and millions of dollars were poured into the construction of these systems, designed to help us keep track of what the Russians were up to. These DEW and White Alice sites are still in place in Alaska, but with the dramatic changes in technology and international relations over the years, they are no longer in use.

John and I shared a few more meals and movies with the air force contingent, watched the ice floes roll by, and kept checking the weather situation in Nome for some indication that Captain Ellerbe and his team were on their way. Finally, after more than a week of waiting, at about eight o'clock one morning, the *Pathfinder* arrived.

Chapter 4

Passing the Test

As ordered, John and I reported to Commander John C. Ellerbe as soon as he came ashore. He had five or six men from his team with him. I must admit, his appearance surprised me. The commander was a soft-spoken man and slight of build—about five feet and eight inches (170 cm) and probably no more than 140 pounds (63 kg). Not at all the rugged-looking individual I had expected to find heading up a project of this scope in the Alaskan bush. But then, looks can be deceiving.

Commander Ellerbe turned out to be one of those rare men who can command attention just by entering a room, without saying a word. I saw this happen again and again that summer, even when the room was filled with raucous men. It's hard to explain, but I think he had an aura of dynamic energy that people responded to. You could see it in his eyes: an intelligence, a liveliness. When he spoke, his quiet words exuded confidence and authority. Yet, there was no sense of arrogance or pretension. He was what my mother would have called "down-to-earth."

The commander wasted no words in getting down to business. He explained the nature of the mission. He and his sixty-man crew were mapping the last half of St. Lawrence Island. They had mapped the first half the previous summer. John and I would back up the survey teams by flying supplies and equipment to where they were needed. Because the weather had delayed them, we needed to get up and running as soon as possible.

Commander Ellerbe spread a map and some aerial photographs out on the table and pointed to the location of the selected campsite along the Fossil River that would serve as a base for the survey teams. The *Pathfinder* would get as close to the spot as possible, but first they were planning to stop at the village of Savoonga, about thirty miles (48 km) east of Gambell on the north coast, to hire some Eskimos from that village to do the lightering of all the supplies from the Pathfinder into the campsite in their umiaks. After that, the ship would leave, and the camp would be on its own. The commander estimated this would take another two days, so he told John and me to meet him and his team at the campsite around noon of the second day.

First thing in the morning, two days later, John and I said goodbye to our friends in Gambell and slid our planes back into the water. The summer sun had done its work; the melting snow had made the lake a good bit larger on takeoff than it had been on landing.

Three or four times during that morning's flight, I found myself slipping back and forth over the international date line, into tomorrow, then back into yesterday. The idea was amusing, until I remembered the Cold War and the Russian airbase, just across the water. These little crossovers were putting me into Russian airspace, a situation that could be fraught with all kinds of complications if the Russians spotted me.

John and I reached the Fossil River and followed it inland. Because of the climate, St. Lawrence Island doesn't have a single tree on it. Flying over it is like flying above the timberline in the high mountains. There are a couple extinct volcanoes in the center of the island, lots of tundra and grass, and a few scrubby little bushes, but from the air it is a very bleak-looking place. About three miles (4.8 km) into the river, the campsite unfolded below us. The surveyors were already setting up their tents on the gravel bed of a small stream left dry when the snow melted.

From a pilot's point of view, Commander Ellerbe had selected the perfect spot for his camp: far enough inland to avoid the sea's heavy winds, but where the river was still wide enough for a safe landing. (Just south of the camp, the river rapidly grew narrow and shallow.) I reckoned the width of the river in front of the camp to be three or four wingspans wide, or about a 150 feet (45 m) across. The grass-covered banks were some 15 to 20 feet (4.5–6 m) higher than the water. The width and depth of the river made landing our planes relatively simple, but John and I were presented with a challenge when it came time to secure them. While the Fossil is a tidal river, its tides don't play by the rules. That's because it has a symbiotic relationship with the Bering Sea. And the tides in the Bering Sea, unlike the tides of most of the world's oceans, do not rise and fall predictably with the pull of the moon. The main influence on the height of its tides is the erratic, frequently turbulent winds generated over the icy body of water. Since the tides on the Fossil River are equally unpredictable, John and I decided to tie down our airplanes at a halfway point out in the water. This way, the Cubs would neither be too far from the shoreline when the tide went out, nor out where the water was too deep to reach them when the tide came in.

Our airplanes secured, John and I began putting up our tent, careful to select a spot that would not upset the symmetry of the camp's design. All the living tents were in straight lines, ten across, with the tent that served as Commander Ellerbe's office positioned in the center.

The walls of the eight-foot-by-eight-foot (2.4-m-by-2.4-m) pyramid-shaped, two-man living tents came up from the ground vertically about three feet (.9 m), then sloped inward and upward to the top of a single tent pole in the center, giving even a six-footer like me ample space to stand up comfortably by the pole to put on his pants. The pyramid shape enabled the tent, when tied down properly, to withstand strong winds from any direction, something for which I was most grateful on numerous occasions that summer. With the flap down, the tent not only protected the inhabitants from the harsh elements, but also from the giant mosquitoes that frequented the area.

Each tent was equipped with two cots, two Coleman lanterns for reading and a Coleman stove for heat while dressing in the morning, for boiling water for tea or coffee in the evening, or for your once-a-week bath. The stove also came in handy for drying your socks, something you found yourself having to do constantly in that climate, no matter how many extra pairs you brought. Any furnishings beyond this required ingenuity, of which there was no shortage in the camp.

The main source of raw material for constructing additional items of comfort was the sturdy wooden cases in which the cans of

Blazo were packed. Blazo was used to fuel the Coleman stoves and lamps. As quickly as the cans were used up, sometimes even before they were used up, the cases would disappear, to reappear a short time later in a tent, transformed into a chest, or chair or table. As the camp took shape, more and more little piles of unboxed Blazo cans began appearing.

That the men under Commander Ellerbe's command showed such exceptional resourcefulness is not surprising. Geodetic survey work in Alaska presented special challenges. Their resourcefulness was a key element in their selection for this project.

First, there was the land itself: marshy, mucky tundra, bordered by sandy beaches, spits, inlets, shallow lagoons, shoal waters and sometimes, as in the case of St. Lawrence Island, rugged mountains to add to the challenge. Then there was the time constraint. Most of the area was inaccessible for surveying except during three months in the summer. Even then the weather was far from ideal. The days were gray and rainy at least 60 to 70 percent of the time, with the temperature ranging usually in the forties (4–10°C). Occasionally, on a good day the temperature might reach sixty degrees Fahrenheit (15°C). The operations were often handicapped by strong winds, heavy fog and persistent rains. To ensure that every occasion for good weather was used to its best advantage, the Coast and Geodetic Survey maintained a policy that only experienced engineers and support crews who knew how to work and survive in this inhospitable terrain were assigned to their Alaskan projects.

I knew a little something about surveying, but I had never worked with a triangulation team before. In triangulation, the area surveyed is measured using a network of triangles. These triangles are determined from a baseline, the distance of which is carefully measured. Angles from the ends of the line are measured to a third point, closing the triangle. The corners of this triangle are then used to locate other points, closing other triangles, thus creating the network. The areas covered are surveyed in as much detail as is necessary to support any activity that will use the information.

Each geodetic survey point determined by this triangulation process is marked with a bronze triangulation mark, which has known latitude, longitude and plane coordinates. To establish triangulation marks that will remain rigid for many years in soil that is mucky in the summer and subject to frost-heaving in the winter, requires special procedures. The bronze triangulation marks are brazed to the tops of metal pipes, which are long enough to penetrate below the permafrost ground level, usually about six feet (1.8 m). Holes for sinking these pipes into the frozen ground are made with a portable device consisting of a long metal pipe through which steam is forced from a small steam boiler.

Responding to my curiosity, Commander Ellerbe showed John and me how he and the project's chief mathematician used trigonometry to determine sites from the angle readings the surveyors got in the field with their theodolites. The theodolite, invented sometime around the sixteenth century by English mathematician Leonard Digges, is a survey instrument that measures vertical and horizontal angles. The commander explained the complex measuring process.

First, the surveyors would insert the brass marker into the tundra or rock. Then they would build a stand over the top of the marker and another stand around the outside of it. They would put their theodolite in the center stand and themselves on the outer stand, to get some distance to make up for the curvature of the earth. If they were working during the day, they would put another marker over the top. At night, they would use a lamp, so that the next surveyor down the line could see their location. The teams had no radios. Every station in the field had a lantern keeper who communicated with the other stations in the field using Morse code.

Six two-man teams were sent out to do the triangulations, usually working ten miles (16 km) at a time. They would set themselves up on top of mountain peaks or other sites from where they could see the greatest distance. The back two men would always move out in front, in leap-frog fashion, as the teams worked their way forward, until the entire segment to be mapped had been covered. Their grid of triangulation would be matched up to aerial photographs and fed into a machine down in Portland, Oregon, called a stereoplanograph, which actually drew the maps. I was eager to see the process in action.

About midmorning on my second day at the Fossil River camp, I was summoned to Commander Ellerbe's tent. He wanted me to fly him back to the *Pathfinder*. He said he had some business to take care of aboard the ship before she left that afternoon. That suited me fine. It was good flying weather; it would have been a pity to waste it on the ground.

"You bet, sir. Be glad to," I said, and we headed for the airplane. I had already checked the oil and the floats, and ensured that I had at least one full tank and one partial tank of fuel. We seldom filled both tanks. The airplane could carry thirty-six gallons (162 l) of fuel which, at six pounds (2.7 kg) per gallon, makes 216 pounds (97 kg) of fuel. If you could fly and get your job done with 100 pounds (45 kg) of fuel, you were a lot better off. You could carry 100 more pounds (45 kg) of freight and take off easier, and your airplane would perform better.

Commander Ellerbe got in the backseat and I taxied out into the river. I checked the Cub's mags and carburetor heat, making sure that all the temperatures were in the green, and took off following the river. The river wasn't straight, but it wasn't too bad; it had just a small curve as you took off.

It was a fairly good day for St. Lawrence. Visibility was probably twenty-five miles (40 km) and the ceiling was 2,000 to 3,000 feet (600–900 m). There was a gentle wind blowing of maybe five to eight miles (8–13 km) an hour. I turned to the east and slightly north, found the shoreline, and flew along it for approximately thirty miles (48 km). Sure enough, out in the water down at the base of the big promontory of Northeast Cape, where the mountain went a little more than 1,000-feet (300-m) high, there was the *Pathfinder*, anchored.

The *Pathfinder* had a displacement of 2,000 tons (two million kg). Her overall length was 229.3 feet (68.8 m). There was ice all around the bow and sides of the ship. Because of the way the wind and the current were working, the anchor was held fast on the bottom and the ice was breaking over the anchor chain, running against the bow, then back along both sides of the ship. But there was still a pond of open water behind it, probably three times as long as the ship—600- or 700-feet (180- or 210-m) long—and approximately seventy-feet (21-m) wide. It tapered out, then back in as the ice went together at the end of the ship. The commander asked me if I thought I could land there. "You bet," I told him.

To make sure, I flew by and counted the number of seconds to double check my estimate of the length, and to see the way the wind was blowing. The conditions were almost perfect for getting the Cub off in a very short run. "No problem, sir," I said. "We can get in behind her." Then I came back around, made sure there were no floating objects in my flight path, and landed.

As I landed, the wind was blowing past the ship. It pushed the airplane backward, away from the vessel, making it easy for me to taxi up to the Jacob's ladder that hung over the side at the stern, which was about fifteen-feet (4.5-m) high to the first deck. The way the wind was blowing, there was no danger of the Cub going under the stern, so I tied the right float to the ladder.

"You're welcome to come aboard if you like," the commander said. The current and the wind were slowly moving the ice from the ship's bow to the stern, but it would be a while before this would create any problems. The plane would be safe enough for now without me, so I took the commander up on his offer.

The captain invited me to join him and Commander Ellerbe for lunch. Wow! I thought to myself as I followed the commander to the ward room—this is the way to live. Just tie your plane up to the back of a 220-foot (66-m) ship and pop aboard for lunch with the captain. I listened, fascinated, as the commander and the captain discussed the summer's projects, when the *Pathfinder* would be back to pick up the survey team, and what the commander would do if we needed more supplies or fuel, or had any emergencies.

After lunch, one of the ensigns took me on a tour of the ship. I got to see the engine room, the cabins and the facilities. The *Pathfinder* was a hydrographic vessel, ideal for the work it did. The crew could take it into a harbor or near shore, lower their small boats, measure the depth of the water, come back on board and plot their data. The ship's ample hold was perfect for storing supplies for ground parties.

When I complimented the ensign on his ship, he told me, with more than a little pride, about the *Pathfinder*'s outstanding service in the Pacific when it was taken over by the navy during World War II.

"And according to Admiral Chester Nimitz," he said, "the road to Tokyo was paved with *Pathfinder* charts." This was a reference to the fact that much of the technical expertise for the naval war in the Pacific was provided by Coast and Geodetic Survey officers transferred into the navy.

When I got back from my tour, Commander Ellerbe was ready to leave. We walked back to the stern, but when we reached the rope ladder, he paused. He looked down at the Super Cub, bobbing in the water, then out across the ice.

"Well, Huntley, think you can get us out of here?"

"You bet, sir!" The ice hadn't changed much since we landed. There was about the same size pond back there.

"How are you going to do it?"

"Well, I'll just untie the airplane and let the wind blow us backward a bit, until we get back to the far end of the pond. Then we'll fire up and take off, and I'll just come toward the ship and go around one side."

I wondered at the time why the commander seemed so concerned. It all seemed pretty routine to me. The takeoff and the flight back to camp went smoothly.

When we landed, much to my surprise, the commander hung around to watch me tie up the Cub. He bombarded me with questions, inquiring about the "what" and "why" of every step of the procedure. I was flattered that such a busy man would take that much interest in me and my work, but all that unexpected scrutiny was a bit unnerving.

When we reached the base, another curious thing happened. The men had finished setting up camp and, except for a few stragglers, they had all retired to their tents to relax. Trailing a few steps behind the commander as he strolled leisurely down the center of the camp toward his office, I noticed that every time we approached a tent, heads would pop out, and the commander would give the men a thumbs-up signal as he passed and a reassuring, "He'll be okay." He repeated the signal and the words again and again as we passed through the camp. The men seemed clearly relieved.

I assumed the commander was referring to someone from the survey team who had gotten sick or had been hurt. I figured that he had seen the man, or received news of him, while he was on board the *Pathfinder*. It wasn't until many weeks later that John put me straight. The "he" Commander Ellerbe was pronouncing "okay" was me. The little excursion to the *Pathfinder* had been a ruse concocted by the commander to check out this "green kid" Nat Brown had dumped on him. There was no way he was going to trust the life of any of his men to me until he was personally convinced that I knew what I was doing. I didn't blame the man. I was, after all, just twenty years old, and he knew I had no bush experience. His team faced enough challenges that summer without adding an incompetent pilot to the mix.

Among those challenges, of course, was the weather, which

turned out to be particularly bad that summer; the worst summer weather the natives had seen in years. The men found themselves weathered-in 40 percent of the time. The terrain that had to be mapped also presented a greater challenge than the previous year. And then there was the isolation. Until the *Pathfinder* returned at the end of the summer, the camp's only link with civilization was a UHF radio in Commander Ellerbe's scientific tent. Theoretically, the commander could use it to contact the Coast and Geodetic Survey or, in the event of a dire emergency, Nome. The only problem with that was that the radio seldom worked.

Still, in spite of these formidable obstacles, the job proceeded smoothly. Commander Ellerbe was a cog that set all wheels into action. He was a graduate of the Citadel and carried impressive credentials in science and mathematics. More important to this assignment, he was an outstanding manager with a gift for maintaining a clear vision of the overall mission, while keeping the individual members of his team focused on the details of their specific jobs. His system was simple: At the end of each day, he would get the men together. Without fanfare, he would ensure that everyone knew what the project was for the next day, and their part in it, clarifying any questions that might arise. The following morning, the men simply went out and got the work done.

One of my jobs was to pilot Gerald "Pinky" Randall, the geodetic engineer assigned to do reconnaissance on the project. Pinky, a pleasant, good-natured chap, was Commander Ellerbe's right-hand man, responsible for the placement of the brass markers. In other words, he was the one who determined where the surveyors would set up their equipment.

I would fly Pinky over a hill or ridge, trying to get him as close as I could to a prospective site, so he could make sure that the surveyors would have a clear, unobstructed view of the next ridge. Getting Pinky on the ground to check out the site meant finding a suitable lake to land on. There was no shortage of lakes on the tundra, but not all of them were suitable for landing.

There are two critical questions a bush pilot needs to answer before deciding whether to risk a landing on a tundra lake: Is there a long enough expanse of water to get in and, more importantly, out safely, and is the water deep enough to support the floats? I had plenty of experience answering the first question. It is a matter of counting seconds during a flyover. The answer to the second question proved to be more complicated.

One important key is color. If a lake is a kind of milk-chocolate brown, it usually has a sandy bottom. If that milk-chocolate brown lake is not very large, a wise bush pilot will avoid it because it will probably be no more than three- or four-inches (7- or 10-cm) deep. However, if the milk-chocolate-colored lake is fairly large, it just might be deep enough to land on. But what you really want to look for is a lake with dark brown water. This is an indication that the lake is probably between three- and ten-feet (.9- and 3-m) deep, a pretty safe bet for landing. This method of judging lakes based on color and size usually works—but not always.

On one of my flights with Pinky, I located a little lake close to an area to be surveyed. The lake was big enough to get in and out of without a problem and the water was dark brown, a good indication that it was deep enough. But when I touched down, I found that I couldn't get the Cub off the step. It tilted up and slid along the bottom, finally stopping with its nose just a few feet from the shore. This time the dark brown water turned out to be only about two-inches (5-cm) deep. To further complicate the situation, the bottom was so mush-soft that when Pinky and I tried to walk ashore, we sank in to over the top of our boots.

A quick word about those boots. One of the first things I purchased for this adventure was a good pair of waterproof hip boots. No sensible bush pilot would fly in Alaska without them. But that summer, out in the far reaches of St. Lawrence Island, I learned that even a good pair of hip boots was no insurance against perpetually cold, wet feet, a chronic condition I endured (along with mammoth-sized mosquitoes) that entire summer. My boots kept the water and snow out all right, but the airtight, waterproof design and material that kept the elements out, also set my feet sweating within two hours. My sweating feet quickly turned my socks into a cold, sopping mess. I was glad I had listened to my cousin Bob, and had taken along plenty of extra socks.

But back to my bottom-beached Cub. Since we couldn't get to shore to turn the plane around with a rope, we had to figure out another way to disengage ourselves from our muddy dilemma. Pinky climbed up and, moving hand over hand, made his way as far out on the left wing strut as he could. This put more weight on one float than the other, enabling us to pivot the plane around until it faced out over the expanse of water. With the Cub properly positioned, Pinky climbed back in, and I was able to take off. John Gallagher, however, wasn't quite so lucky on his first encounter that summer with the deceptive lakes of St. Lawrence Island's tundra.

Chapter 5

A Pilot Missing and Other Adventures

One day John Gallagher went missing. The weather was good, the flight was routine; he had just gone on a short run to pick up one of the surveyors and bring him back to the main camp. It should have only taken a couple hours. So when dinnertime came and went without any sign of John and his passenger, I became concerned. The Cub had no radio. If John was in trouble, there was no way he could contact the camp to let us know.

Still, I wasn't too worried. I knew that if anyone could handle an emergency landing on this unforgiving terrain, John could. He was a topnotch pilot and mechanic, and he seemed to thrive in the bush. He even looked the part of the quintessential bush pilot. He was about five feet and ten inches (175 cm) tall, a solid 180 pounds (81 kg), and had coal-black hair so thick and coarse that there was always a bluish cast to his chin, even right after he shaved. But in spite of my confidence in John's ability to handle an emergency, I was relieved when Commander Ellerbe finally called me and the camp's two helicopter pilots to his tent around nine o'clock that night and announced that it was time to start looking for the missing Cub.

The two 'copters assigned to the camp represented brand-new technology in 1951. In fact, Commander Ellerbe was one of the first people to use helicopters for field work on one of his jobs two years earlier. The helicopters did the same work the Cubs did, only they did it at a much higher cost. The government was paying fifty dollars an hour, plus gas, for the Cubs. The helicopters were 300 dollars an hour and used considerably more gas. The commander used them frugally—only to reach sites the Cubs couldn't reach, areas where there were no lakes nearby to land on. But, when the safety of any man in his charge was at risk, the commander mobilized every resource at hand.

Fortunately, there was still a good bit of daylight left. I took off and flew a grid pattern back and forth over the campsites and wherever else I thought John might have gone. Dick Sherman, one of the surveyors, went with me. I was grateful for the extra pair of eyes. Even with Alaska's lingering summer daylight, a silver Cub downed on snow in overcast weather would not be easy to spot.

We scoured the tundra for nearly five hours, but could find no sign of John's airplane. Dick and I headed back to camp. It was about two o'clock in the morning when we landed; we had no more light and were almost out of gas. The commander was waiting for us. The 'copters hadn't had any luck either. Commander Ellerbe sent us to bed with instructions to pick up our search again after we had gotten some rest.

I dozed off, tossing and turning for about two-and-a-half hours, but real sleep was impossible with John and his passenger stuck somewhere out there on the tundra. So I fueled up the Cub, packed some sandwiches, collected Dick, and took off again. Fortunately, the weather was holding up.

I remembered a big lake, about five-miles (8-km) long and three-miles (4.8-km) wide, near where the Morrison-Knudsen Company had set up its construction camp. Morrison-Knudsen was the contractor that had been hired to build the radar station. A big lake like that would be a natural place for a bush pilot in trouble to head for.

As I approached the lake, I spotted something gray at the edge. Sure enough, it was John's Super Cub. It was sitting in about three inches (7.5 cm) of water. I could tell because John and his passenger were standing, ankle deep, next to it. They were talking to two men on shore. The two men turned out to be Pinky Randall and one of the helicopter pilots. They had spotted the stranded Cub about twenty minutes earlier and had set the 'copter down on the closest piece of dry land they could find. As I flew over the lake, I saw that the water was a chocolate brown, but seeing how big that lake was, it should have been deep enough to land on. Obviously, John must have come to the same conclusion.

I opened my window and put down my flaps. Pulling the power back, I buzzed the grounded Cub. John waved up at me frantically and shouted something, but his words got lost in the sound of my engines. I waved back and continued on around to land on one of the little dark ponds about 100 yards (91 m) from the edge of the big lake.

"What were you yelling at me?" I called across the water to John as Dick and I joined Pinky and the helicopter pilot on the edge of the lake.

"Not to land here!"

I had to laugh. Did he really think, after seeing the trouble he had gotten himself into, that I would do anything that dumb? But then, John never seemed to expect me to have good sense. Perhaps it was my youth or my lack of experience. No matter how well I performed, he always seemed to hold on to some doubt about what would happen the next time.

The problem now was how to get John's Cub back in the air, but he had already figured that out. He sent me back to camp to pick up six two-by-sixes, about twelve-feet (3.6-m) long, and some stakes. John's plan was to make a slide track out of the two-by-sixes, which he would use to get his Cub into deeper water so he could take off. I tied the two-by-sixes to the outside of my float struts, threw a bunch of stakes into my baggage box, and returned to the lake.

Dick and the helicopter team helped me dismantle my cargo and carry it out into the lake. Standing ankle deep in the water, we rocked the Cub back, slipped one of the two-by-sixes underneath the keel of the float, and slid the airplane on top of it. There wasn't very much water touching the floats, probably no more than an inch (2.5 cm) to an inch and a half (3.75 cm). Then we put another two-by-six down in front of the Cub and drove some stakes into it to hold it down, taking care to put the stakes deep enough into the wood so that they wouldn't bump on the floats and puncture them. We repeated the process with the next two-by-six, and the next, until we had constructed thirty-six feet (11 m) of skid out in front of the stranded Super Cub.

While we were laying down the skid track, John pulled a reed out of the sandy lake bottom, siphoned all of the gas out of the Cub, then poured five gallons (23 l) back into the left tank. He turned his fuel selector to the left and climbed into the backseat, so his center of gravity would be aft. Putting on his takeoff flaps, he told us to hold the airplane fast until he signaled us.

The wind was blowing right at the airplane at about ten to fifteen miles (16–24 km) an hour. This gave John a good headwind to work against. He got the throttle all the way up and signaled us by dropping his hand. We let go and held our breath as John skidded over the thirty-six feet (11 m) of boards in front of him, hit the water … and finally climbed into the air. As he turned and headed toward camp, we reclaimed the valuable two-by-sixes from the bottom of the lake and reattached them to my float struts. Then we all climbed into our respective aircraft, with John's stranded passenger hitching a ride with the helicopter team, and took off for camp and some much needed sleep.

One of the most challenging and critical parts of survey by triangulation is the measuring of a baseline. The baseline is a mile-long horizontal line that must be measured with special precision, and serves as a foundation for all the other measurements. It was the first thing the surveyors did. To do it, they had to locate a level area one-mile (1.6-km) long. Once they found their level area, they put stakes in the ground 100 feet (30 m) apart. Using a special tape, which they placed on top of the stakes, and a finely measured weight, they would pull on each end of the tape so that the slack between each stake was consistent. Then, using little brass marking strips, they would mark the exact distance of 100 feet (30 m) on top of each stake. They did this, one stake after another, until they completed the measurement of the mile.

There were a number of things they had to take into consideration as they worked. The wind couldn't be blowing more than five miles (8 km) an hour. The outside air had to be within a certain temperature, because the temperature would affect the length of the tape and even whether the stakes remained solidly in the ground. Any movement would throw the surveyor's measurements off. With these precautions, they were able to get an accuracy of within one tenth-of-an-inch in one mile.

The only feasible location to put in the one-mile (1.6-km) line turned out to be on the other side of the island from the team's Fossil River base camp. For four intense days, John and I ferried supplies, tents and men to the far side of the island, about forty miles (64 km) each way. After the outlying campsites were set up, we continued to fly in supplies and carry back progress reports for the commander.

Once the baseline was measured and the survey locations were selected, John and I started carrying the men and their materials and equipment, including their tents, out into the bush as quickly as possible, so the surveyors could get right to work. After the first week, the flights became routine. We would pile the two-by-fours we needed by each float, then tie a stack of them about two-feet (.6-m) high on each of the float's struts. As long as we limited our fuel to just what we needed to make the trip, the Cubs were able to handle this load and anything else we needed to carry in the baggage compartment.

The work days were long and intense, and there was little in the way of amusement back at the base camp, so it was not surprising that when Kelly, the cook, found a little arctic fox pup, the new addition received a lot of attention from everyone. Kelly fed the pup well and built him a run out of some wire. He did his best to domesticate the little fox, but never really did succeed in taming him. That was probably just as well. Once the job was over, the little fellow would have had to learn to fend for himself again. As it turned out, after about a month and a half of putting up with his human captors, the fox broke his tether and headed back into the wilderness, without so much as a backward glance.

Maybe only other pilots can understand what I mean when I say that I feel the most alive when I'm flying. I can't imagine what my life would have been like if I hadn't been able to spend so much of it in the air. Flying for Commander Ellerbe and his "merry men" that summer was as good as flying gets. Every day brought new adventures, new challenges, new things to learn, all of which was always fun. On top of that, never before or since have I felt more appreciated, but then I have never flown in a place where an airplane was more important.

Let me give you an example: If I could get a survey team into a pond close enough to where they wanted to put in their survey marker, that ten-minute flight probably saved those men a whole day's worth of trudging through the tundra. The key to being able to do this, of course, was finding lakes that we could operate out of. With a small or light load, we were able to get in and out of a 1,000-

foot- (300-m-) long lake very easily. In smaller lakes, it took a little bit of wind and some good approach or departure areas so that we could take off over grass instead of trying to go up a hillside.

John and I also got used to flying at a very low altitude. When the weather was good, we would fly high on the way to the site because we could see farther from that altitude and therefore spot the tent, the lake or the location that we were going to more quickly. But, on the return flight, we would immediately start working our way back at a low altitude so that we would know what the terrain looked like from fifty feet (15 m) or less. That way, when the weather turned bad, we would know the land well enough to be able to fly with reduced visibility clear down to a mile, or sometimes even less. This practice paid off for me numerous times. One of those times involved a trip to the baseline camp.

We hadn't been able to get out to the baseline camp for about three days because of bad weather. This left the camp dangerously low on food and fuel. Since it didn't look like the weather was going to clear up any time soon, Commander Ellerbe asked me if I thought I could get through. I agreed to give it a try.

I loaded up the groceries and the fuel and took off about ten o'clock in the morning. It was a foggy, misty day—one of those days when even the grass looks gray. But the wind wasn't blowing very hard. I picked up an old familiar route. On this particular compass heading, there wasn't anything higher than 100 feet (30 m) in the air all the way across the island. Pretty soon the weather got down to where it wasn't reasonable to stay in the air any longer, so I touched down in a lake that I knew was there, even though I couldn't see it until I came right up to it. I pulled up on the shore and pulled out my book.

You never went flying out in the bush without a pocketbook or two. My preference was a good western or adventure novel. I also enjoyed a good detective story. It was during my summer working on St. Lawrence Island that I discovered the "Sam Spade" series. I would pull out my book and read for a while, looking out the window periodically to check the weather. If the weather improved, I'd fly another few miles until the weather was bad again. By the time I worked my way across to the far side of the island, it was almost four o'clock. I flew out over the Bering Sea, turned left to the east and followed the shoreline toward the baseline camp.

The water was a beautiful shade of blue. I was looking down into that blue water, admiring it, when I spotted the strangest thing. At the bottom, some 100 feet (30 m) down, in the mud, there was a series of dots and dashes. It looked as if someone had laid down a message in Morse code. I wondered who, or what, had caused those marks. Then I got my answer. Up came a giant blue whale, the biggest living creature on earth. He blew spray in the air as I flew right over him. His tail flukes were wider than the wingtips on the Cub. It was a thrilling sight!

I continued to work my way down the beach, passing by the entrance of a lagoon that I knew was about a mile and a half (2.4 km) from the camp. I couldn't see the camp, but because I was familiar with flying low over this ground, I knew where I was. The camp was actually on a little lagoon within this lagoon, an area completely cut off from the rest of the lagoon, but right on the edge of it. I saw the edge coming up, went over it and touched down on the water. The camp came into view.

The survey team at the baseline camp was pretty happy to see me, or, more accurately, to see the Blazo fuel I had brought. They had run out that morning. The commander had been right about their food rations, too. They were almost gone.

I must admit that my knees were knocking just a bit as we unloaded the Cub. All those hours of intense flying in low visibility had taken its toll. In the air, I had been too busy concentrating on where I was going to notice the stress. Now that I was on the ground, it really hit me. I was exhausted. And since the weather didn't look like it was going to break any time soon, everyone agreed that I should spend the night.

After supper we played cards for a while, then I was shown to an empty cot in one of the tents and I settled in for the evening. I read for a little while and was just about to turn out my light when the tent flap opened and there, standing in the entrance, was John Gallagher. This was about some four hours after I had landed, around eight-thirty or nine o'clock at night.

Now, like I said, John and I got along all right most of the time, but he did have a tendency, on occasion, to treat me like a recalcitrant son.

"What are you still doing here?" he demanded. "Why didn't you fly back to base camp?"

wing. If I had had a radio, I would have immediately reported them. I kept watching them, trying to figure out what I would do if they buzzed me or got too close. When this didn't happen, I began to think about how I would report this when I got back. I noted down my exact location, my compass heading and the probable position of the UFOs from me. Suddenly, they changed again: the three became two, and then four.

Now this was all pretty heady stuff for a twenty-year-old newly initiated bush pilot. I'm heading back to base camp trying to document everything I'm seeing when, all of a sudden, in the location where I spotted the UFOs, I saw the edge of the clouds and the moon behind it, all kind of orange, fairly close to the horizon. That's when I realized that my UFOs had been nothing more than the moon shining through cracks in the clouds. But I'll tell you, for those ten or fifteen minutes, it was all very exciting.

Throughout the summer there was a real feeling of camaraderie in camp, but by August I noticed that the mood was beginning to change. Tempers flared. Men who were usually easy-going and friendly became impatient and testy. The weather, the strenuous work, the isolation and boredom had begun to take their toll. I even found myself getting a little "bushy," which might, in part, explain why I reacted so violently to Wimpy's little prank that August morning in the cook tent, although there were those who thought Wimpy had it coming.

Wimpy was a tobacco-chewing mechanic with a thick southern drawl from, I believe, Tennessee. He had been hired to keep the Weasels running. This versatile piece of equipment not only had tracks that enabled it to climb the most formidable hills with ease, but its rear propeller and waterproof hull made it fully operable in water. It was the ideal transportation for the wetlands and tundra of St. Lawrence Island. Like the Cubs and the helicopters, the Weasels provided an essential lifeline for the surveyors.

As I said, it was Wimpy's job to keep the Weasels running, but his personal and professional style left a good deal to be desired. Especially what he referred to as his easy-going nature, which most of us around camp viewed more as a case of plain, old-fashioned laziness. For example, there was the way Wimpy put up his tent. All of the other men built floors for their tents, but not him. He preferred gravel under his feet. If he put in a floor, he said, he'd have to spit

I told him the truth. I didn't think it was safe to fly.

"Well, I just flew in."

I got up and looked out the tent opening. There were our two Cubs parked side by side, but, as far as I could see, the weather hadn't gotten any better. I told John I still didn't think it was safe to fly and suggested that he spend the night, too.

"I've got to get back and tell them where you are."

That's when I realized that Commander Ellerbe had sent John to look for me. I guess when I didn't show up back at camp that evening, he got worried. No wonder John was annoyed to find me safe and sound and settled in for the night. He turned on his heels and headed out of the tent, but stopped at the entrance and glared back at me.

"Well?"

"Well what?"

"Aren't you coming?"

"No."

Uttering a few choice swear words under his breath, he stormed out of the tent. A few moments later I heard him take off.

I had a lot of respect for John as a pilot, but there were times when I didn't agree with his judgment. This was one of those times. In fact, I thought to myself, I should probably keep an eye out for his parts and pieces on my way back to camp the next morning. But John had a real knack for bad-weather flying. He made it back to camp that night. If he had any problems, I never heard about them.

That whale I spotted on the way to the baseline camp that day was one of the highlights of my summer, but it wasn't my only memorable sighting on St. Lawrence Island. UFOs were a great topic of conversation back in 1951. That year, sightings had been reported all over the world, from Minneapolis to New Delhi. There was even one that month (June) in Niagara Falls. So one evening, as I was coming out of the baseline camp at about dusk (ten or eleven o'clock at night) and saw this glowing cigar-shaped object flying parallel with me off to my left, I was sure I knew what I was looking at. It was a fair distance off, but going at my speed. I had never seen anything like it before. It had to be a UFO.

All of a sudden there was what looked like fire dripping from it and then another "ship" appeared below it. And a few moments later there was another one. So there I was, with three UFOs off my left his tobacco into a can and throw it away every morning. This didn't make any sense to him when he could just spit it out right there on the ground. Didn't care much for bathing either, which, by the end of the summer made it difficult for anyone caught downwind of him. But the main complaint we had about Wimpy was the way he did his job.

Wimpy subscribed to the theory of "least effort." When he repaired a Weasel, he would take it apart down to the part that was broken. If he decided that the part was essential to the operation of the vehicle, he'd fix it; otherwise he'd just throw it away. He would then put the vehicle back together again. During that process, if he found any other parts he didn't deem critical for the operation of the vehicle, he'd just leave them out. By the end of the summer, he had a whole pile of discarded parts sitting in his work area.

One day, while he was reassembling one of the Weasels, Wimpy came across the plugs for the two tanks that made it possible for the Weasel to float on water. Deciding they were unnecessary, he tossed them on his "extra parts" pile and finished putting the Weasel back together. The next day two of the surveyors headed off in that Weasel to check out an area across the Fossil River. They started across, but the further into the river they got, the deeper the Weasel sank. By the time they reached the other shore, the Weasel was sitting on the bottom. It was a good thing the river wasn't any deeper at the time.

The two surveyors got the Weasel halfway up the riverbank when it stopped dead. The water that had seeped into the unplugged floats made the floats so heavy that the Weasel couldn't move. So there they sat for about half an hour, until enough of the water had slowly leaked out of the front float to allow them to move up a little more. Then they sat for another half an hour as the water trickled out of the rear float. All the while they waited, they sputtered angry words of advice to the absent Wimpy; they advised him to go home and take up a new line of work. When I learned about their problem, I dug the plugs out of Wimpy's parts pile and taxied them across the river in the Cub, so the men could re-cross the river safely on their way back.

But, back to the cook tent incident. I always took off at eight o'clock in the morning, so, about ten minutes to eight, I would go into the cook tent for breakfast. That morning the tent was crowded;

all three tables, which held eight men each, were full. I had a special agreement with the cook, Kelly. He always cooked up one very large pancake for me, so large it filled my whole plate. That morning, as I took the plate from Kelly and turned to go, I walked smack into Wimpy.

"Lookie at what this here boy's got," Wimpy jeered, tobacco juice dribbling out of his mouth. Then he skewered my pancake in the very center with his greasy, dirt-stained thumb and pulled it right up off the plate.

At that point I guess I just lost it. "Give that back!" I yelled and, without thinking, gave Wimpy a great push. He fell backward into the tent pole. Kelly leaped for the gas stove and shut it off, just in the nick of time, as the whole tent collapsed around us. I untangled myself and, with a barrage of angry voices ringing in my ears, crawled out from under the tent and headed for my plane, without my breakfast. Having to listen to my growling stomach all morning further fueled my anger.

For the next three days, Wimpy and I managed to avoid each other. We probably would have continued our squabble for the rest of the summer if Commander Ellerbe hadn't intervened. On the fourth day of our feud he called me into his tent.

"We've got some parts down in Gambell. I want you to take Wimpy down there to look at them, to see which ones we need, and fly them back here."

In hindsight, I realize that there was no urgency to this trip. Commander Ellerbe could have put it off all summer without any adverse effect on the project. What the commander was really concerned about was camp morale. Two feuding members of his team were not good for that morale.

It was about a 100-mile (160-km) flight from the Fossil River to Gambell, and the commander knew that by the time we flew there and back, Wimpy and I would be talking again. Of course, he was right. We not only started talking, we even found things to laugh together about. The feud was over.

At the edge of a lake about midway between the outlying camps and the main camp, a four-man party was constructing a wooden tower over one of the benchmarks. I had struck up a special friendship with two of the men on this team, Smitty and Eli. On my way back and forth to deliver supplies to the outlying camps, I got into the habit of dropping in on my friends to see if they needed anything, or sometimes just for a cup of coffee and a little conversation. To break up the monotony of my routine, I would occasionally play a prank on them.

One of my favorite tricks was to buzz their camp early in the morning. I wouldn't go directly over their heads. That would have put them in jeopardy. I would fly to the side and make a little noise, just to make sure they weren't sleeping in. One morning, feeling a bit more adventuresome than usual, I decided to go between the two tents. They were far enough apart that I wouldn't be directly over anybody, but close enough to give them a little scare. As I flew between the tents, I heard a strange "PINGGGGG," but didn't think much about it. That is, until I made my turn around to land in the lake and found four fellows out there waiting for me, all shaking their fists. I had cleared the tents all right, but my floats had taken out the aerial wire between the two tents, seriously disturbing the men's morning radio listening. It took some fancy talking and a promise to replace the aerial, which I did the very next day, but they finally forgave me. You can bet I never tried that little maneuver again.

Things had been going so well that summer that I must admit I was becoming a little cocky. I began to think I could do no wrong. The snagged aerial was the first chink in my false sense of invincibility. The second came a few days later.

Smitty and Eli's team had finished their work. The morning they were scheduled to shut down and move back to the main camp, the weather turned bad. It was closing in quickly. Concerned that my friends and their teammates might get disoriented in the deteriorating weather, I headed for the site to see if I could help. By the time I got there, the camp was already gone, but I could make out two pairs of Weasel tracks heading out. The problem was, they appeared to be heading toward the northwest—the wrong direction. I had to find the team and turn it around before the men got lost.

The weather continued to roll in. Even flying low, I was having a hard time keeping the Weasel tracks in sight. Finally, ziiipp! First one and then the other Weasel went by under my wings. I tried to signal them with a wing dip, but they just waved back and kept on going. I tried again, with the same results. In an effort to make them understand their mistake and get them turned around and headed back in the right direction, I flew out ahead of them and started a right turn. Suddenly, through a break in the mist, I saw it, right there, directly below me—the center of the main camp. The survey team wasn't lost … I was. I continued over the camp and landed on the lake. You can bet I never said a word to anyone, but the incident sure took the air out of my overinflated ego.

Chapter 6

The Big Blow and the Bungled Beef Caper

On July 12, 1951, the barometer suddenly dropped and the wind picked up to about twenty knots. There was no doubt about it, a good size storm was moving in. John and I headed for the river to secure our airplanes. Because of the Fossil River's unpredictable tide, we always tied the Cubs to stakes, but it was going to take more than a couple of stakes to keep them from blowing away if the storm hit at gale force.

We filled the floats with water and tipped the planes forward until the front of the floats were about knee-deep in the river and the back of the floats were slightly out of it. Then we filled some empty fifty-gallon (225-l) gasoline drums with water and tied them tightly to the wing hold-down fittings, pulling them taut. The barrels floated slightly, but they would become heavier and heavier as they were lifted out of the water when the wind tried to lift the planes. To keep the planes from moving around in the water, we put in a second set of stakes. Then we tied the stick forward in the cockpits. This way, when the wind attempted to lift the plane, the elevator would make a nosedive and the plane wouldn't lift off. Finally, we put a two-by-four just back from the leading edge of the wing at about the center lift, to spoil the air flow over the wings. This would also prevent the wind from lifting the aircraft.

The work was wet and strenuous and took us about three hours. By the time we were done, the wind was shrieking by us at forty-five to fifty knots. If it kept building at this rate, even all our precautions might not be enough to keep the Cubs in one piece; however, there was nothing else we could think of to do.

The campsite itself was well protected by the tundra, which rose some fifteen feet (4.5 m) above the gravel streambed, on which we had raised our tents. This, of course, was no accident. Commander Ellerbe had just such weather in mind when he had selected this site for his main camp. Once we had everything properly tied down, there was nothing much for us to do. Except, that is, for the cook, who, storm or no storm, still had to provide three hot meals a day. The rest of us retired to our tents.

With the wind outside now whipping through the camp at about seventy to eighty knots, it was impossible to maintain heat inside the tents. To stay warm, we hunkered down in our sleeping bags and read, wrote letters or tried to sleep—which, believe me, was no easy feat with all the thunderous flapping going on around us.

About midday, I crawled out of my sleeping bag to refasten a loose tent flap that was driving me to distraction. When I reached the entrance to the tent, I happened to glance outside in the general direction of the communal latrine, which, for practical purposes, had been situated downwind of the tents on a piece of high ground with suitable drainage for such a facility. The privy was a two-holer. A lot of work had gone into making it stout and sturdy so that, even out in the open as it was, it would be able to weather a bad storm. But just as I glanced in that direction, a sudden gust of wind came barreling down the tundra and plucked the latrine's tent right up off its foundation, hurling it over the hill and out of sight, and leaving the privy's single occupant, a surveyor from Arkansas named Hill, unceremoniously exposed for God and all the world to see. Except for the look of amazement on his face, sitting there, bare-bottomed, his elbow poised on his knee and his palm supporting his chin, he could easily have been the model for Rodin's celebrated statue, "The Thinker."

The unrelenting wind continued to blow off the Bering Sea for the next two days, with gusts sometimes peaking as high as eighty-five knots, or more than 100 miles (160 km) an hour. Three times a day, we would bundle up, duck our heads behind our elbows and thrust ourselves into the wind, to fight our way to the cook tent for a hot meal. Then it was back again to our flapping tents and sleeping bags.

By the third day, I had myself a severe case of cabin fever. Charlie, one of the surveyors I had befriended, came to my rescue. He popped his head into my tent and asked me if I wanted to go for a ride on the Weasel. The wind had abated slightly and Commander Ellerbe wanted someone to check on the tide gauge, to see if it had survived the storm. I was in my parka and out of the tent before Charlie finished his sentence.

Some 500 feet (150 m) above us, the broken clouds were blowing by so fast that I felt like we were moving even before we took off. The spot we were headed for was about three miles (4.8 km) away. Charlie put on the windshield wipers. It wasn't raining, but the fast-moving north wind blowing down out of Nome had picked up a lot of water as it passed over the Bering Sea, and a spray some twenty- or thirty-feet (6- or 9-m) high smashed into our windshield as we drove.

We found the tide gauge in good order about 200 yards (182 m) from the shoreline. When the commander's team analyzed the information, we learned that the wind from the storm had piled the water up so high on the north side of the island that the tide had reached an all-time high for that summer.

As soon as the storm was over, John and I rushed to the river to check on the Cubs. Thankfully, our precautions had worked. The planes had taken a beating, but they had come through without any structural damage. We pumped the water out of the floats and informed the commander that we were ready to fly. He immediately put us back to work. He sent John to check on the surveyors in the outlying camps and dispatched me to the Morrison-Knudsen camp at Northeast Cape. "Make sure they're okay," the commander instructed me, "and whatever they need, you take care of it."

When I landed on a little pond near the Morrison-Knudsen construction site, the camp's director, a man named Nielsen, came out to meet me. Nielsen was a small, rugged man, about five feet and eight inches (170 cm) tall, with a round, gray stubble beard and black sideburns.

"We're okay," he assured me. "Just some minor damage, but nothing serious. However I'd appreciate it if you could do us a favor. We're out of fresh meat."

The camp was supplied by navy landing ship tanks (LSTs), which were moored on the other side of the island. When it came time to replenish the camp's supplies, one of the LSTs would make a run down around the bottom of the island and up to the camp. However, the storm had upset the schedule. Even now that it was over, it would still take the navy a couple days to load up and make the trip. That meant that the camp would have to go without fresh meat for two or three more days. With fifty hardworking, hungry men to feed, Nielsen had a serious problem. He asked me if I would make a run over to the ships and pick up a side of beef to tide them over.

"You bet," I said. It was a simple enough request: thirty minutes there and back, maybe another forty-five minutes, an hour at the most, to load up. We shook hands and I was on my way.

My estimation of the time it would take to get there was right on the nose. It took me exactly fifteen minutes over tundra and mountains to reach the Bering Sea on the other side of the island. I spotted a large lagoon about a quarter of a mile from where the LSTs were tied together on the ocean side, and continued on to make a pass over the ships. The three ships had anchor gear out at the bow and stern to prevent them from swinging around. The wind was blowing the ships to the east, so I turned and came at them from the same direction, landing right behind the last one. As I taxied up closer and shut off my engine, an ensign appeared at the rail, some fifty feet (15 m) in front of me and about fifteen or twenty feet (4.5–6 m) above me. I opened my window and called up to him.

"The director of the Morrison-Knudsen camp says they're running short on meat. He asked me to pick up a side of beef for his construction crew."

"Fine," the ensign called back. "But the meat is two ships over—the one farthest to the west. I'll tell them."

So far, so good. I let the wind blow me back, took off and headed for the lagoon. I found a suitable spot on the shoreline, touched down and pulled my airplane up, pointing the nose to the north, away from the beach. I figured that it would probably take the navy about forty-five minutes to get the side of beef loaded on the landing craft and to shore. When I saw them coming I would just climb over the sand dunes to the beach and meet them. In the meantime, as always, I had a good book to read.

Every once in a while I would look over my shoulder to see if the landing party was on its way. Half an hour passed. Then an hour.

I could see plenty of activity aboard ship, but no sign of a boat between ship and shore. Another thirty minutes passed. Something had to be wrong. I fired up the Cub and headed for the most western ship, the one on which the beef was stored. There was a landing craft personnel (LCM6) next to it. it. A fifty-six-foot (17-m) twin-screw, welded-steel craft with forward cargo well and bow ramp, and it was filled with frozen beef, and more beef was being loaded into it. The sea was too rough for me to come alongside, but I could get in fairly close if I went between the anchor chains off the stern. I touched down.

"Hey, wait a minute," I called to an ensign helping to load the beef. "I can't carry all that! All we need is one side of beef." The ensign shrugged his shoulders. "Well, that's really too bad," he drawled. "The beef's unloaded and it's coming to shore."

Before I could argue the point, someone fired up the beef-laden craft and headed for the beach. I jumped back into the air, landed on the lagoon and ran down to where the LCM6 had come ashore. The sailors were carrying the beef to thirty or forty feet (9–12 m) from the shoreline and just dumping it in the sand.

"Wait a minute!" I called, frantically waving my arms. "I can't take all this. All that's going to happen is that beef's going to spoil."

"We're just doing what we were told, son," one of the swabbies answered, as the men kept piling the beef up on the beach.

I threw up my hands in defeat. It was clear that nothing I could say would stop them. Hefting a quarter of beef up on my shoulders—it must have weighed at least 100 pounds (45 kg)—I staggered up through the sand to my plane and dumped it in the back. Then I staggered back down and got one more quarter, and took off for the construction camp.

"We've got a problem," I told Nielsen as the construction workers unloaded my cargo. He listened as I explained what happened, nodded his head and said, "Hmm." Worried that the man didn't grasp the gravity of the situation, I tried again.

"Look," I said, "those Seabees have piled up somewhere in the neighborhood of seven or eight tons (7,000–8,000 kg) of beef on that beach. The payload of the Cub is only 400 pounds (180 kg), maximum. It would take me forever to transfer all that meat."

"You can't get the plane any closer?"

"No, sir. The sea's too rough. But that's not ..."

"Tell you what we'll do," Nielsen interrupted. "You can't load all that beef by yourself. We'll give you a couple of our Eskimo construction workers here, and you fly them over and have them bring the beef up to the lagoon."

I'm not sure how it happened, but before I knew it, I was off with two Eskimo helpers to ferry seven or eight tons (7,000–8,000 kg) of frozen beef from the other side of the island to the camp, a couple hundred pounds at a time. After about eight trips, and some four hours of flying time, both the Cub and I were running out of gas. I looked at the pile of beef on the beach. We had hardly put a dent in it. Commander Ellerbe had told me to do anything I could to help out the construction team, but I was sure that the commander hadn't anticipated anything of this scope. I made a decision. I told the two Eskimos to get into the plane and headed for Northeast Cape.

All the way back, I went over my argument in my head. I had to make Nielsen understand that what he was asking wasn't feasible. First of all, I was running low on gas. More importantly, I had to get back to the Coast and Geodetic Survey camp and my own projects. I'm sure Nielsen knew what was coming as soon as he saw the Eskimos get out of the plane. Before he could say a word, I launched into my argument. Much to my surprise, the objections I anticipated from Nielsen never came. He simply nodded his head.

"Of course," I said, shaken by his stoic silence, "I'll ask Commander Ellerbe for permission to finish ferrying the meat, but," I quickly added, "with our tight schedule, I seriously doubt if the commander can afford to spare me any longer."

Nielsen smiled. "I appreciate what you have done, son," he said. "Why don't you just take this quarter of beef back with you to camp."

It was a whole hindquarter, and it made me an instant hero. Even the commander came out of his tent at the sight of me marching down the center of the camp toward the cook shack with 100 pounds (45 kg) of frozen beef slung over my shoulder. No one was happier to see that hindquarter of beef than the cook, who hadn't had any fresh meat to serve the men in more than a month. It is hard to say which the men enjoyed more, the fresh meat or my tale of how I got it. When I finished my story, and the laughter subsided, the commander got up and patted me on the back. "Good job, son," he said. "Well done."

But that wasn't quite the end of the "Bungled Beef Caper." Morrison-Knudsen also had some air support, a Grumman Goose they kept based in Nome, 110 miles (176 km) from Northeast Cape. The Goose flew every day that weather permitted, but the pilot only gassed up on Mondays and Thursdays. When the Goose arrived at Northeast Cape the next day, which was a Thursday, and Nielsen asked the pilot to fly over and pick up the rest of the beef, the Goose had nearly a full tank of gas.

The size and configuration of the Goose made it perfect for the job. And, by this time, the Bering Sea had calmed down. The pilot was able to land on the ocean side of the island and taxi right up on the hard-packed beach, almost next to the pile of beef. This made loading a snap. With the Goose's ability to carry a ton or more at a time, the mound of beached, frozen beef quickly disappeared. However, the combination of large payload and short runs meant the Goose was burning some fifty or sixty gallons (225–270 l) of gas an hour, a fact that for some reason failed to register with the pilot. Accustomed to fueling up only on Mondays and Thursdays, it didn't occur to him to check his fuel the next morning (Friday) before taking off again for Northeast Cape. When I arrived at the Morrison-Knudsen camp about nine o'clock that morning to deliver some paperwork from Commander Ellerbe, I found a worried Nielsen waiting for me.

"We've got a Mayday," he said. "Our Goose is down in the middle of the Bering Sea. He got halfway here and ran out of gas."

It took me about twenty minutes to get back to the Fossil River camp and relay Nielsen's request for a search, which, of course, Commander Ellerbe granted. I found a bunch of empty five-gallon (22-l) cans and filled them two-thirds full with gasoline. This way, if I found the Goose and couldn't land, I could drop the cans in the water and they would float high enough so the pilot could retrieve them.

With thirty gallons (135 l) of extra gas aboard, I set out for Northeast Cape. From there I picked up a compass setting for Nome. Leaving the island behind me, I headed out over the seemingly endless Bering Sea. The weather was overcast and rainy; visibility was about four miles (6.5 km). I reckoned that I would have to go out some forty or fifty miles (64–80 km) to find the Goose. In terms of time, that would take me about thirty to thirty-five minutes out on my search pattern. With no radio or navigational equipment, and no landmarks or for that matter land, to guide me, I had only my watch and my compass to keep track of where I was.

I flew for thirty-five minutes, then turned for about three miles (4.8 km) and turned again on a new track back toward St. Lawrence Island. I flew for fifteen minutes in this direction, then turned and turned again, heading back toward Nome for another fifteen or twenty minutes. I flew this pattern for two-and-a-half hours, back and forth, back and forth—searching the horizon for some sign of the Goose, without success.

Somewhere in the middle of the Bering Sea, about twenty minutes into my third hour and headed toward Nome, I checked my fuel. It was clear that unless I wanted to risk becoming the object of a search myself, I had better head back.

The southern route back toward St. Lawrence Island seemed to take forever. Visibility was now about two or three miles (3–5 km) at most. I kept a nervous eye on my fuel gauge. I had that extra thirty gallons (135 l) of gas aboard, but to use it, I would have to land. Looking at the choppy water below, I crossed out that possibility. My Cub didn't have the Grumman Goose's advantage of size and weight to survive a water landing in these conditions.

Finally, after about forty minutes of flying, just as I was beginning to think I'd never find St. Lawrence Island, I spotted land. As I got closer, I realized that I was considerably west of my destination, which, of course, made sense since I had been flying an east-to-west search pattern. It took me another twenty minutes to get back to Fossil Lake. I landed with about forty minutes of gas left in my tank.

I got some good experience in ocean search flying that day, but in the end, credit for rescuing the downed pilot went to a tug boat that happened by around six o'clock that evening, with enough gasoline aboard to get the Goose back to Nome. After bobbing up and down in the middle of the Bering Sea for some ten hours, it's a good bet that that pilot never again chanced taking off without first checking his fuel gauge.

Chapter 7

Weather and Waves

A s I said, it wasn't the terrain or the work but the weather that always presented the greatest challenge on St. Lawrence Island that summer of 1951. I don't mean the temperature, which ranged between thirty-four and forty-eight degrees Fahrenheit (1–9°C), or even the rain. They were no different from what a pilot would encounter flying in a normal Seattle winter. The problem was the fog. St. Lawrence Island has a maritime climate. When a heavy fog rolls in, which happens frequently, it sometimes stays for days. If the fog was thick and down on the deck, we were grounded, but if it was intermittent, we would often attempt to fly. That decision frequently put John and me in situations that tested both our ability as pilots and our knowledge of the territory.

There was this one time that we had been fogbound for four days. All work was at a standstill. Finally, on the afternoon of the fifth day, the weather showed signs of clearing. Eager to get things moving again, Commander Ellerbe asked John and me if we thought we could get two of the surveyors over to their next camp in the flat tundra country. The site was on the edge of a lake about twelve miles (19 km) from where the Morrison-Knudsen camp was set up. The job involved a lot of equipment, which meant a couple of trips, but John and I decided to give it a try.

When we reached the site with our first loads, the lake was still partially fogged in. We landed in the clear part and taxied up to the fog-shrouded shoreline. As quickly as possible, we dropped off the gear and turned around to take off. At first, all we could see in front of us was fog. We waited. The minute we spotted the sun burning through, we gave it the throttle and leaped off the water. But it was apparent, as we headed back to camp, that the fog was on the move again. If we wanted to get the surveyors and the rest of the equipment in, we'd have to hustle.

Back at base camp, John and I picked up the two surveyors and the remaining equipment and headed out. John got off the water first. I took off ten minutes later. By the time I reached the lake, it was more than half covered with fog. John was already at the shore, almost unloaded. He took off as I pulled in beside him. I finished unloading, turned the Cub around and headed back to our base camp. It was twilight. The sky was robin's egg blue, turning toward dark. And the fog had begun creeping in from the Bering Sea. It kept on creeping, all the way up to the Fossil River.

I knew when I had reached the base camp because I could see our little outhouse perched on top of the hill. But that was all I could see. The rest of the camp and the river below were hidden by the fog. With his ten-minute lead, John had been able to slip in before the fog got all the way down to the deck, but it was solidly down there now. You can't land on a river you can't see.

I weighed my options. I could go further up river and look for a clear spot, but there weren't many landing places further up the Fossil River. Even if I could find one, I'd have a hard time taxiing back down to camp in that fog. While I couldn't see the river, I could see the hills around it, and I knew the gorge was only twenty-feet (6-m) deep. I decided to fly between the hills, right over where I knew the river had to be, to the spot where I wanted to land. Maybe I'd get lucky and find a break in the fog.

Flaps down, my nose in the clear sky and my tail in the fog, I flew down the river. I flew a straight line as if I was going to land but, of course, I didn't try. I was some fifteen feet (4.5 m) in the air and couldn't see anything beneath me.

When I pulled up and made my turnaround, I saw that my flaps had made a deep groove in the fog, blowing it away right over the spot where I wanted to land. What a piece of luck! I had found a possible solution to my dilemma. At least one worth pursuing.

Keeping my flaps down and my nose up, I oriented myself to the sunshine and made another pass, this time in the opposite direction. The edges of the fog flew by. Pulling up again and looking back, I could see the water. I made one more pass, this time deeper down in that groove, but always careful not to lose my horizon or my visibility. Now I could see the river and the shoreline. And something else. There on the shore was our entire team. They had heard my engine and had come out to see what I was up to.

I would like to take credit for thinking up this ingenious fog-dispersing technique, but as I said, I just stumbled on the idea. And it was a good thing that I did. If I hadn't figured a way to get in that evening, I would have had to land on a pond somewhere and wait until the fog lifted, which, as it turned out, didn't happen until late the next day.

One day, Commander Ellerbe and his crew decided they wanted to put in a geodetic marker on a point of land on the shoreline about halfway between the Fossil River and the Northeast Cape Morrison-Knudsen camp. It was going to take three surveyors and 400 or 500 pounds (180–225 kg) of equipment to get the job done.

On my first trip, I took one of the surveyors along, a fellow named Tom, as well as some bags of cement, the geodetic markers and a rock drill. It was a pretty full load. The surveyors were going to install their marker on a jagged pile of rock jutting up from the beach. Now, ocean landings can be rough, especially along those flat beaches where the large ocean rollers come crashing into shore. I had flown over the area earlier to check it out. Based on my experience, I decided that the waves striking this beach were small enough to be manageable. They weren't pounding the shoreline; they just reached up on the beach two or three feet (.6–.9 m), then slipped back down again.

I touched down and rode into shore on the back of a wave. This is what you normally do when you've got any kind of sea swell. I learned this lesson from a flight instructor I had when I was at Kenmore in 1947. The gentleman had landed a Taylor Craft out by Clallam Bay and was taxiing into shore when he somehow got on the front side instead of the back side of a wave. He found himself upside down on the beach with the swells from the Straits of Juan de Fuca pounding the airplane apart. Fortunately, he and the fellow with him got out without any difficulty—if you don't count getting wet. But his misjudgment finished off the flying machine.

As I moved in toward shore, I noticed that there wasn't any wind blowing. That was the good news. A lack of wind reduced the chances of the plane rocking. The Cub, if you remember, was 1,500 pounds (450 kg) on 1,400 floats, which made it just a little under float at its gross weight. This configuration made working ocean swells or waves a little tricky. When landing and turning toward shore, you had to be careful how you maneuvered the airplane. You didn't want it to rock and put one wing down deep so that the float would go under on one side.

The bad news was that because of my lack of experience, I seriously miscalculated the situation during my reconnaissance of the area. The waves were bigger than I had anticipated. A lot bigger! What I hadn't realized was that the shoreline was steep. The waves weren't crashing onto the beach because they were breaking on this steep slope before they ever reached the beach. However, at this point, there wasn't anything I could do but try to make the best of the situation.

I called to Tom in the backseat and told him to get out on the float and, the minute we touched shore, jump off and grab hold of the wing strut and turn the airplane around. As I said, we were on the back side of the wave, so the wave broke just ahead of us. I maneuvered the Cub up to where it touched on the gravel and Tom jumped down into about six inches (15 cm) of water. But before he could grab hold of the wing strut, the next wave hit. Suddenly he was standing almost waist-deep in water, with a surprised look on his face that was priceless. I jumped down and took hold of the wing strut on my side. Each time a wave hit and picked us up, we turned the plane.

A few minutes later, John Gallagher came in with his fellow and freight. We discussed the situation and agreed that conditions were borderline. However, we already had more than half the people and most of the equipment there. We might as well finish the job.

I helped John unload and got back in my Cub. Every time a wave came in, it would lift the airplane, then set it back down on the gravel. I started up the engine. When the next wave hit, I applied the power and taxied out. The waves seemed even steeper moving away from shore. The tail just about touched the water before the airplane finally made it over the crest. There were a couple times I wasn't sure it was going to make it. I had this vision of myself, flipped over and bobbing helplessly in the water, floats up, while the waves dismantled my airplane. Fortunately, that never happened. I finally made it out to where the waves were no longer influenced by the ground effect of the shoreline, which enabled me to turn around and take off.

Bringing in the other surveyor and the next load of equipment was basically a repeat of our initial experience. The afternoon flights with the remaining equipment were a little easier, however, because we weren't carrying as much weight.

I learned an important lesson from that experience: When you are working in open water, don't trust your eyes. The signals you see aren't always accurate indications of the way things are. Eventually, as I gained more experience, I learned how to spot a steep shoreline and always factor in that information when I am trying to judge the size of waves by the way they are hitting a beach.

As August progressed, the days grew shorter. Sunset and sunrise became more clearly defined. The middle of the night was now dark. Less sunlight meant less flying time, and the less I flew the more restless I got. But I wasn't alone. The surveyors were also getting "bushy." The work had been intense and challenging, but for more than three months now we had been living in tents with few amenities, miles from civilization. We were all ready to go home. Finally, the word came: the triangulation was completed and its accuracy confirmed.

The confirmation of the surveyors' data had been a monumental task. Every night, by gaslight, often while the rest of us slept, Commander Ellerbe and Smitty had poured over the field reports, analyzing and checking all the figures. This was in the days before computers. All the calculations had to be done manually, using volumes of trigonometry. When the last figure in the last report was verified, the commander sent John and me and the two Kern Copter pilots off to pick up the men who were still out in the single tent camps around the island.

One of those men was a chap known as Red. Red was somewhere in his late forties or early fifties. He was a whiz with the theodolite and no one could top him when it came to communicating in Morse code. But Red was an alcoholic.

All summer long, Red had kept his problem under control. He had this bottle of whiskey in his suitcase, which flew everywhere with him. But he never opened it, not once during that entire season. Not until that August evening when the helicopter went to fetch him back to the base camp for the last time.

With his campsite cleared and his equipment and belongings safely on board the helicopter, Red pulled out his bottle, filled up a cup and drank it down. He continued filling that cup up and draining it all the way back to camp. By the time the helicopter deposited him at the main base, he was soundly soused. From that point on, until he boarded his commercial flight in Nome for the trip back to the States, I don't believe that man drew a single sober breath.

Red wasn't the only one who celebrated the end of the summer by tying one on. Kelly, the cook, had been making up a batch of home brew for most of the summer, a concoction he created out of pear, peach and apricot juice and any other sweet juice he had available. He stored the juices in a butter barrel to let them ferment.

Now, I was just twenty, remember. I hadn't had much experience with alcohol, but I knew a little bit about brewing alcoholic beverages from fruit juice. My step-grandfather, Bob Levesque, was a tavern owner. When prohibition came along and put him out of business, he turned his tavern into a milkshake shop, but it was his lucrative side business that paid for the family's luxuries around the holidays. Bob Levesque sold cherry juice, a *very special* cherry juice. During prohibition, selling and transporting alcohol was illegal, but having and drinking it wasn't. My grandfather devised a way to freeze cherry juice so that it remained juice during his transactions and delivery. But as the juice defrosted and "aged" in the customer's backyard woodshed or other storage area, it mellowed into a fine cherry wine. During the prohibition years, Bob Levesque's cherry wine was enjoyed at Thanksgiving and Christmas dinners all over Puget Sound.

Of course, Kelly wasn't aiming for a genteel holiday wine with his brewing project. He finally brought it out for our farewell party the night before the *Pathfinder* was scheduled to pick us up. The elixir was a little syrupy, but it had an indisputable kick. A couple glasses were all I could handle, which was fine. The surveyors certainly didn't need any help from me to finish off the contents of Kelly's butter barrel. That evening I detected a definite correlation between the shrinking level of the liquid in the barrel and the rising good spirits of the men.

The next morning, the surveyors faced their final challenge of the summer. Hangover or no hangover, it was time to pack up. They moved from task to task like zombies, but the job got done.

When the *Pathfinder* arrived, Nat Brown was on it. He had come to help us disassemble the Super Cubs. Nat was sure that after a summer workout in the Bering Sea, the two airplanes would be in no condition to make the long flight over water. His plan was to take them apart and load them onto the ship, which would take them to Nome. You can imagine his surprise when he found both Cubs in excellent shape. They looked almost as good as they did the day they left Seattle. That was because John and I, being mechanics as well as pilots, had meticulously kept up our 100-hour inspections and made all necessary repairs. Nat was so pleased with the condition of the Cubs that he decided to forgo his original plan and fly them out.

"In fact," he said to me, "your plane is in such good shape, I think I'll fly it over to Unalakleet myself." I was to go on to Nome on the *Pathfinder* with the survey team, then take Alaska Airlines down to Unalakleet, pick up the Cub and fly to McGrath.

That's when I learned that my summer job wasn't quite over. Nat still had some work left for John and me to do. He sent John to join a group working on the Yukon River. I was to finish out the season flying out of McGrath with a party that was doing some reconnaissance work in the central part of Alaska.

I had no objections to going to Nome on the *Pathfinder*. The idea of sleeping in a stateroom after a season of tent living sounded to me like real luxury. Nome was about 110 miles (176 km) away. The trip didn't take very long. I got on the boat that night, had a good night's sleep in my state room, a good breakfast the next morning, and I was there. As soon as we were docked, I headed for the airport to pick up my airline ticket for Unalakleet, but the flight for that day was already filled. I would have to spend the night in Nome.

The surveyors, still in a celebrating mood, headed over to the Bering Sea Club and its well-known watering hole, the Bering Trading Company Bar, where, they confided, there were some native women waiting who would be very happy to see them. They invited me to join them. I politely declined. At twenty, I had not yet mastered the art of partying, and women, especially older, more experienced women, made me feel ill at ease. The great passion of my life at that time was airplanes. I was eager to see what beauties I could discover out on the airfield.

I was most intrigued by the older planes, like the derelicts left by Pacific Northern Airways, an early aviation pioneer in Alaska. There was a tri-motor Stinson with all the fabric off, just sitting there, and an old Hamilton that was a corrugated miniaturization of the Ford Tri-motor. That plane had been part of the Wein Airways operations for many years. There were a lot of Stinson Reliants around the field, the kind of airplane that got me so excited on those family trips to Boeing Field when I was six or seven. These Reliants were still active, still flying into the bush out of Nome, carrying freight and passengers ... everything from dog teams to fuel oil, to keep the economy of that region going.

I know the surveyors partying at the bar wouldn't have understood, but for me, wandering around the Nome airport that day, talking to pilots, finding out where they flew in from and where they were going, telling them about what I had been doing, was much more fun than any drinking party could be.

Nome itself was another amazing discovery. The Victorian buildings that had been constructed at the turn of the century were built on permafrost. The term "permafrost" means permanently frozen. However, this doesn't preclude partial meltdown from time to time, which, unfortunately, doesn't make permafrost a very good foundation. As the permafrost melted beneath the buildings, the buildings began to tilt. When you looked down the well-surveyed streets, what you saw was a bunch of buildings, some lived in, some abandoned, all at crazy angles from one another.

The dowdy old Victorian houses with their odd angles and their lace curtains reminded me of a bunch of tipsy old ladies leaning up against one another. They made the perfect backdrop for the surveyors I ran into on my way to the hotel. They, too, as they moved along the street from bar to bar, were tilted slightly off-center.

My flight was scheduled to leave at eight o'clock the next morning, so that evening I searched out Commander Ellerbe to tell him how much I appreciated being able to spend the summer with his party. They had certainly treated me well. He nodded and said that he hoped to see me the next summer. The commander was a man of few words. I took his comment to mean that he liked the job I had done for him. The fact that it came in the form of an invitation to work for him again the next summer made the compliment that much nicer.

Chapter 8

Unalakleet, McGrath and Home

The next morning, I showed up at the airport bright and early and hopped aboard a C-46 headed for Unalakleet, 148 miles (237 km) southeast of Nome. The scheduled run, operated by Alaska Airlines, also made stops at Kotzebue, Bethel and Anchorage. Aviation buffs will remember the C-46 as the old DC-3 Curtis Commando, the biggest two-engine transport the military used during World War II. In its airline configuration, this tail dragger (so-called because it had its third wheel below its tail) carried somewhere around forty to forty-five people. We all rocked, rattled and rolled inside the cabin as the airplane thundered down the runway and lifted off into the air, with its two big old R-2800 Pratt & Whitney engines groaning and belching smoke.

Once we were airborne, I got to thinking about Nat and my Cub. Unalakleet is located on Norton Sound, at the mouth of the Unalakleet River. To get there from St. Lawrence Island, which is directly across the Bering Sea, Nat once again had to fly more than 100 miles (160 km) over open ocean by himself and out of the sight of land most of the time. Even after my open-ocean flying that summer to get to St. Lawrence Island, I still found the prospect daunting, but I knew that for Nat, it was just another routine flight.

Unalakleet, like most of the places we worked out of that summer and the next, had no road access. The small Eskimo village still doesn't today. The only way in and out is by airplane or boat, which makes a fairly recent archeological find there all the more remarkable. What the archeologists have uncovered are remnants of houses along the beach ridge that date from between 200 b.c. and a.d. 300. This means that in spite of its weather and remoteness, the area has supported some form of a community for more than 2,000 years. This is probably because Unalakleet sits at the terminus of the Kaltag Portage, an important winter travel route connecting to the Yukon River. As a result, it has been a major Indian and Eskimo trading center over the years.

In 1901, the United States Army Signal Corps ended Unalakleet's isolation from the western world by installing more than 605 miles (968 km) of telegraph line from St. Michael to Unalakleet and over the Portage to Kaltag and Fort Gibbon. Next came the airplane. But I saw no evidence that these technologies had any impact at all on the day-to-day life of the native population. The main occupation was still fishing. The only other industry I saw was the gathering, spinning and hand-knitting of the underwool, or quiviut, from a herd of musk oxen the villagers maintain just outside of town. My first visit to Unalakleet was a brief one. By the time I got there, Nat was already gone, leaving the care of my Cub in the capable hands of Art Johnson.

Art was an Eskimo pilot who worked for Alaska Airlines. He flew a Norseman. Every day, on floats in the summer and on skis in the winter, he would make a round-trip flight starting in Unalakleet. Art would fly down past St. Michael, going south and then across the mouth of the Yukon Delta to Bethel, picking up freight and passengers in the small villages along the way. In Bethel, Art would connect with one of Alaska Airline's big C-46s or C-47s. After transferring any outgoing and incoming passengers and freight, he would head back to Unalakleet, making any necessary stops along the way.

Anxious to get to my job in McGrath, I thanked Art for his help and hospitality and took off, flying up the Unalakleet River and across the mighty Yukon. And mighty that river is. At 1,979 miles (3,166 km), the Yukon is the third longest river in North America and, in some places, more than a mile wide. But it is its wandering course that I find so remarkable; the way it goes all the way from the Bering Sea, north across the Arctic Circle and then turns and goes south down into Canada. I continued across the hills and mountains between the Yukon and the Kuskokwim Rivers, finally reaching McGrath. The 220-mile (352-km) trip took me four-and-a-half hours.

McGrath is located in the very heart of Alaska's interior, 221 miles (354 km) northwest of Anchorage and 269 miles (430 km) southwest of Fairbanks. Named for Peter McGrath, a local U.S. marshal, the town began life back in 1907, mostly because of its location, which was at the northernmost point on the Kuskokwim River and accessible by large river boats. It quickly developed into a regional supply center. When the river changed course and left McGrath on a slough, and useless as a river stop, the townspeople simply moved their town.

The McGrath I flew into in the summer of 1951 was built on a loop in the Kuskokwim River. There were no roads connecting to the town (and still aren't). Supplies for the community and the surrounding mining district were brought down river on barges, tugs and stern-wheelers from Bethel, where the big ships from Seattle docked.

The first thing that struck me flying into McGrath, especially after spending most of the summer flying over the desolate, treeless landscape of St. Lawrence Island, was the surrounding hills. They were beautiful. There were towering spruce trees rising forty-, sixty-, sometimes 100-feet (12-, 18-, 30-m) tall. Interspersed among them, the birches, aspens and poplars had turned a bright yellow with the first frost of the year.

The layout of the town's airport was dictated by certain geo-graphical constraints. The "T" part of the airport's runway pointed toward where the loop of land the town sat on and the river con-nected. Part of the mainland went off toward the trees to the south-west. But the main runway was river-bound, running from river shoreline to river shoreline. There was no way to extend it without damming the river. Given the size and force of the Kuskokwim, that seemed to me like an unlikely prospect.

I landed on the water and taxied close to the main runway. The river was a bit frisky that day. The current was running somewhere around three or four knots. To keep the airplane from drifting down-stream, I built a little cairn on the shore, put a stake in it and secured the Cub to the stake. I hoisted my duffle bag onto my back and, checking to make sure that I wouldn't be run down by any arriving or departing aircraft, hiked across the runway to town.

Actually, McGrath wasn't really very much of a town. There was a roadhouse facing the runway. There was Jack McGuire's Bar. And there was this old, long barracks-type building that had been used as a staging area during World War II. That's where the Coast and Geodetic Survey billeted its surveyors and pilots that summer. We would eat in the restaurant and sleep in the old barracks building.

Remember how the pilots in Kipnuk in the beginning of the summer balked at the idea of being replaced by John and me because that would have meant they would lose out on their overtime pay? Well, I was half expecting the same kind of reaction in McGrath, but it didn't happen. It had been a long, hard summer for these pilots. They were tired of flying and perfectly content to just lounge around town and let "the new fellow" do all the flying he wanted. That suited me fine. I was eager to see this new country, although, quite honestly, I couldn't understand how anyone could ever get tired of flying.

For the next two weeks, I got to fly every single day. Commander Ellerbe even hired a guide for me from McGrath, a man who had done some flying for the Coast and Geodetic Survey. He had a Piper P-11 and knew the country. I would fly along with him into some of the lakes. He'd show me where the camp was. Sometimes we would work together, carrying in gear or maybe setting up a couple of surveyors for a short period of time.

Being in the interior, McGrath's weather was much better than St. Lawrence Island's, but flying out of McGrath was not without its challenges. The Kuskokwim is an old river. From time to time it meanders off. Sometimes these meanders would disappear some thirty or forty feet (9–12 m) into the ground, leaving behind a dark, reasonably clear lake. Many of these lakes were shaped like a "U" or a hook. They were deep, but narrow, with vegetation close to the side or floating. You would pull your airplane up to what you thought was the shoreline, only to find when you got there that the shoreline had sunk, and there you were, floating free again.

The trick was to get stopped, grab hold of a little willow bush and tie the float to it so that you wouldn't drift away. Then you would put all your cargo out on your float to organize it, because you didn't want to have to make more than three trips to shore over that marshy ground. With every trip, you'd find the soggy trench made by your footsteps growing deeper and wetter. More than three trips and you risked penetrating through and finding yourself swimming in forty feet (12 m) of water underneath a floating island or some floating muskeg or bog attached to the shoreline.

Sometimes in this area, the height of the trees or the shape of the lake can spell trouble for a pilot. If you aren't careful and go in too far, you might not be able to get back out. I'll never forget the day I flew into one of these odd-shaped lakes, not thinking much about it. I unloaded my cargo. Everything seemed to be going okay—until I looked back to the spot from where I had to take off. A lump formed in my throat.

The lake was about 100-feet (30-m) wide, but my takeoff route looked awfully narrow. That was because the trees on both sides of the lake were taller than the lake was wide. I couldn't shake this vision of my wings all tangled up in those treetops. To clear the trees, I would have to climb up over 100 to 150 feet (30–45 m) on my takeoff. My instinct was to fly right straight down the center line, only there was no center line. I managed to make it out that day, but let me tell you, it was pretty spooky there for a while.

It was during those two weeks of flying out of McGrath that I learned an important lesson about handling aviation fuel. One of the surveyors needed to go to a place on the Yukon River not too far from Ruby. It was a long flight, so we took twenty extra gallons (90 l) of gas on board in four five-gallon (23-l) cans.

The assignment was to fly by some mountaintops and see if we could see the top of the next mountain, so the surveyors could tell where to put their sites the following summer. We flew right down among the tops of the ridges, all the way up to the Yukon. When it came time to refuel, I landed, climbed up on the wing, sat down and poured the extra gasoline into the wing tank. I must have spilled some because when I finished, I discovered that I was sitting in a puddle. It was uncomfortable, but I wasn't too concerned. Especially when I climbed back down and noticed that the wind had evaporated all the gasoline I had gotten on my trousers.

However, on the way back to McGrath, the cockpit got very warm. With each mile I found myself growing increasingly uncom-fortable. It seems that the gasoline had not only gotten on my trousers, but it had penetrated through them to saturate my under-wear. The dampness was annoying, but I still didn't think I had a major problem. Not until the next day. That's when I noticed that the hide was coming off my backside. The skin continued peeling off my behind for a whole week. I was fortunate that I didn't get lead or gasoline poisoning, but that thought brought little comfort as, each day, I climbed into the cockpit, gritted my teeth and delicately eased myself down on my very tender bottom.

Finally, the time came to shut the operation down. Nat had made arrangements to store his Cubs in McGrath for the winter. He was there when we took the airplanes out of the water. We put them on the truck bed of a trailer rig and drove them over to one side, past the Federal Aviation Administration (FAA) shacks, next to where the "T" was in the runway. There we unloaded them and tied them down. As eager as I was to get home, I still felt a certain sadness, a sense of letdown, now that the time had actually come to leave.

Nat handed me my check and said that he hoped to see me again. I looked down at the amount. He had paid me in full for my services, but he had also promised to pay my way back to Seattle. When I asked him about it, he just shrugged his shoulders and said that he was sorry, but we just didn't have a very good season.

I was disappointed. I thought that I had done a good job for him. I certainly had done everything I said I would do. Now he wasn't doing what he said he would do. It wasn't until some years later, when I found myself in a similar position, that I fully appreciated the spot Nat was in at the end of that summer. Just getting all those Cubs up to Alaska must have cost him a small fortune. On top of that, the government only paid him every thirty days. He was still waiting for his final check when the time came to pay us off. That meant the money had to come out of his pocket, which I'm sure must have drained almost all of his available cash. In spite of his good intentions, I realize now that he probably just wasn't in a financial position to keep his word.

The money I had earned that summer was earmarked for my next semester at school. I really didn't want to dip into it to get home. There was a Noorduyn Norseman on floats in McGrath that had been under contract to the Coast and Geodetic Survey all summer. The fellow flying it was Ken Armstrong. I had met Ken two years before down at Kenmore when he was having that Norseman put together. He agreed to let me hitch a ride with him as far as Anchorage.

The weather was down, so we couldn't get over Rainy Pass, which would have put us on the direct route between McGrath and Anchorage. Instead, we kept working our way down the passes toward the west and south. Since the weather wasn't getting any better, and it was getting dark, Ken decided to set down at Iliamna for the night.

Iliamna is on the northwest side of Iliamna Lake, near the Lake Clark Park and Preserve. It's a pretty big lake; in fact it's the second largest lake in the United States after Lake Michigan. When landing on big lakes like that, you worry about what the wind will do. The waves can get tremendous. But in spite of the inclement weather, the water was fairly calm that day, and Ken managed to put the Norseman down without any problems. We pulled the plane up on the beach and I began refueling by hand pump. The Norseman took 150 gallons (681 l) of 80/87 out of barrels. Let me tell you, that took a lot of pumping.

The next morning was pretty clear, but it was starting to look like winter. The sky was slate gray with bits of sunlight breaking through the high clouds. The wind was blowing at about ten to fifteen miles (16–24 km) an hour. Ken got the Norseman fired up right away, but it takes a long time to warm up that R-1340. When it was ready, he pushed the throttle to it, and away we went, off to Anchorage.

Two-and-a-half hours later, we touched down on Lake Spenard. There was a new international airport going up right beside Spenard and its sister lake, Lake Hood. A channel had just been dug between the two lakes so that the seaplanes had a bigger area from which to take off.

Ken and I tied the Norseman down and hailed a cab. Much to my surprise, the driver turned out to be a woman. I had never seen a female cab driver before. But then, I hadn't traveled in many cabs, either. We threw our bags in the back and jumped in. "Westward Hotel," Ken said, and we were off.

About a half mile down the road, Ken tapped the driver on the shoulder and asked, "Where's the nearest whorehouse?" I was glad it was dark. I could feel my face turning beet red. "You're in it," she snapped back, without missing a beat. Kenny smacked his knee and let out a roar. His laughter was contagious. We were both still laughing when we got out of the cab at the hotel.

I never did find out if what the cab driver said was true. I left Kenny on the sidewalk and went in to see about a room. That was the last I saw of him, or the lady cab driver. The next day I boarded a Pacific Northern Airlines DC-4 for Seattle, a little richer, hopefully a better pilot and certainly a lot more worldly.

Chapter 9

The Summer of '52 and the Cub that Nearly Went to Sea

The fall of 1951 found me back at Washington State College in Pullman. I had this dream of owning my own fly-in resort somewhere up north. My summer adventure in Alaska had ignited a new fire under that dream, and I dove into my junior-year studies in hotel administration and resort management with renewed enthusiasm. To earn some extra money and keep my skills sharp, I gave flying lessons through the Throttle Jockey Flying Club in my spare time. One thought energized everything I did: come May, I would once again be heading for Alaska.

November, December and January passed with no word from Nat Brown. I finally heard from him in February. His contract with the Coast and Geodetic Survey had been renewed. "Would you be interested in flying again this summer for Commander Ellerbe?" he wanted to know. It was the question I had been waiting for all semester. I had planned to answer it with what I hoped would sound like an air of professional indifference. But true to character, my excitement overrode my intentions. "You bet!" I blurted out.

However, my enthusiasm for the project didn't stop me from addressing some concerns I had. Maybe it was the influence of my business law class, but remembering the misunderstanding over my return flight at the end of the previous summer, I decided to ask Nat for something that probably no pilot had ever asked him for before—a contract. I just wanted to make sure, up front, that both of us were in agreement on the terms of my employment.

Actually, I had two concerns. Aside from wanting to make sure that Nat would pay my transportation home at the end of the summer, there was also the matter of meals. All Nat's pilots were responsible for their own expenses, which was okay with me. But what had happened the previous year was that John and I were charged 120 dollars a month for food, almost double the sixty-two dollars a month the surveyors were charged. That additional fifty-eight dollars a month represented a pretty big chunk of money back in 1952, especially for a young man trying to work his way through college. I wanted Nat to pick up that fifty-eight-dollar-a-month difference. Other than those two things, I was happy with the rest of the arrangement, which was the same as the previous summer: I would be paid ten dollars an hour, with a guaranteed eighty hours, and the standard overtime rate. I wasn't sure how Nat would react to my requests, but he agreed to everything. I had a lawyer in Pullman draw up the contract. Nat signed it without comment.

When May finally rolled around, I returned to Seattle just long enough to say good-bye to my mom and pick up my equipment at Kenmore. Then I hopped on a Pacific Northern Airlines DC-4 headed for Alaska. In Anchorage, I switched to a DC-3 and flew on to McGrath. The town looked pretty much like I remembered it, except that the big old Kuskokwim River was rolling by with its spring runoff, and the water was close to the top of the banks.

My new partner, Paul Garner, was already in McGrath. He had been there for about a week and a half, helping to change the floats on the Super Cubs. After the previous summer, Nat realized that the 1400-size floats were just too small for the kind of work we were doing, so he was replacing them all with new 2000 floats.

Paul was no stranger to me. I knew him from Kenmore. He had taken his training there under the G.I. Bill, an educational assistance program for the Armed Forces. Paul had been in the infantry in World War II and saw some tough action in New Guinea. He was a likable, easy-going chap, about my height, but a lot slimmer. Like me, he was a mechanic as well as a pilot. I looked forward to working with him.

As each new float installation was completed, the aircraft had to be taken up river and flight-tested. The moment Nat spotted me, he put me to work. One of the planes I got to test was number eight, the Cub I had used the previous summer. Having flown it all season, I

Friends helped Ted celebrate his first solo flight at age 16 with a dunking in Lake Washington.

A chance to fly the Alaskan bush was a dream come true for 20-year-old Ted Huntley in the summer of 1951. The experience set his whole course in life.

One by one, Ted and the five other Cub pilots eased up to the Ellis Airlines's float in Ketchikan, Alaska, the summer of 1951. It was the second refueling stop, on what Ted remembers as the longest flying day of his entire career.

Left: Ted delivering supplies to a survey camp during the second summer.

Below: Even the floats of Ted's Super Cub were used to haul supplies and materials to the outlying camps during the surveying process.

Ted's Super Cub #8 served him well the summers of 1951 and 52 as he flew in support of the Coast & Geodetic surveyors charged with helping to map Alaska.

Empty military weather station housing in Gambell provided temporary housing for Ted and John while they waited for the Coast & Geodetic Survey ship to arrive with Commander Ellerbe.

Ted and John, their first day at the Fossil River base camp on St. Lawrence Island, putting up their two-man tent.

Kenmore Air Harbor in the early fifties.

Tommy McQuillan (right) confers with one of his workmen.

Left: Tommy McQuillan's cabin on Border Lake.

Below: Towing Ted's plane to put on wheels for some prospecting flights in the mountains with Tommy, in British Columbia the summer of 1956.

Above: Looking up the the Salmon Glacier towards the chute near the summit. The other side goes down to Leduc Glacier.

Right: Drilling equipment on Leduc Glacier, searching for a copper deposit.

Above: Ted secures plaque *(right)* honoring Tommy McQuillan on McQuillan ridge, named in honor of the prospector.

Above: Kenmore Air Harbor, 1951, the south end of Seattle, on Lake Washington, where Ted's adventures began.

Left: Commander Ellerbe, who headed up the Coast & Geodetic Survey team Ted flew for the summers of 1951 and 52.
Photo: NOAA Photo Library.

Coast & Geodetic Survey ship, *Pathfinder.*   *Photo: NOAA Photo Library.*

knew it pretty well and was confident that it was in good shape because I knew how hard I had worked to keep it that way. It felt really great to be back in the cockpit, especially on those new floats. It felt so good that I persuaded Nat to let me have that good old number eight again for this new season.

McGrath's night life, what there was of it, revolved around Jack McGuire's Bar. During the day, all the business and money transactions that took place in central Alaska happened around the five or six tables in the back room, but at night, the action was in the bar. That's where all the gold miners, prospectors, surveyors, equipment operators, pilots and other adventurers passing through gathered at the end of the day.

On our last evening before flying out to meet Commander Ellerbe in Unalakleet, Paul and I were seated at the crowded bar with Nat and the other pilots. Our party was also graced by the presence of two very attractive young women, Nat's niece, Valerie, and her friend, Sally, visiting from California. Now remember, McGrath was just a little outpost in the middle of the bush. With the exception of the native population, women were in short supply. So you can imagine the kind of stir these two comely young divorcées created when they showed up in town. Both women were very well endowed, but Sally perhaps a little more so. Her striking figure must have made quite an impression on someone in town. Just outside of McGrath, there are two mountain peaks named for her. No joking.

Anyway, we were all sitting around the bar, having a drink and swapping stories when a husky young man comes in and heads straight for Valerie. She tried to ignore him. When that didn't work, she told him to "take a walk." Her rebuff only seemed to encourage him.

Now, Nat was sitting hunched over the bar next to Valerie. He straightened up and swung around on his stool. Nat was about sixty-two or sixty-three years old at the time, but age doesn't seem to matter very much when you're six-feet-and-five-inches (193-cm) tall and around 280 pounds (126 kg). Reaching over, he grabbed the young man's collar, lifted him clear off the floor and pinned him to the wall, leaving the poor fellow's feet dangling about a foot and a half off the ground. The two men were now eye to eye. Suddenly the room was silent. Nat pulled his left arm back and shook a clenched, ham-sized fist in the young man's face.

"You didn't get that this lady doesn't want to talk to you any-more?" he asked in that booming baritone voice of his. "I'd advise you to get out of here."

"Yes, sir," the young man replied.

Nat nodded and dropped the fellow. He hit the floor with a bang and was on his feet and out the door in a split second.

The young intruder evidently wasn't the only one that night to fall under Valerie's spell. My partner, Paul, couldn't keep his eyes off her. I didn't think much about it at the time. As I said, the young woman was very attractive. She was about five feet and eight inches (170 cm), with honey blond hair, dark eyebrows and great big brown eyes. But I had no idea just how enamored Paul was of her, nor could I have guessed that before the summer was over, his infatuation would trigger an adventure for me. But I'm getting ahead of my story.

The next morning, Paul and I loaded up our Cubs and headed out across the interior of Alaska, across the Yukon and down the valley that leads into Unalakleet. After you fly over the fairly low pass between the Yukon and the Bering Sea (probably only about 1,800- to 2,000-feet (540- to 600-m) high between the peaks), you hit beautiful country filled with big trees. It's an outstanding area, considering it's so close to the Bering Sea where there is nothing but treeless, windswept tundra.

As we approached Unalakleet, the weather wasn't very good, but that was to be expected. Although I had visited the village briefly at the end of the previous summer, to pick up my Cub and fly it to McGrath, I had come in on a commercial flight. This was my first time flying into the area. The village sat on a sand spit. Just behind the sand spit there was an estuary that stretched out about a mile from the river, going north. It was still filled with ice. I was grateful for all the experience I had taxiing on ice and snow the previous summer in Gambell. Paul and I touched down in the part of the river that was open, slid up on the ice and taxied about half a mile until we were close to the center of town, where we pulled up on the beach. This would be our operating base for about half of the summer. Commander Ellerbe and his survey team had come in the day before. Paul and I picked up our tent and cots and got set up. In the tradition of the camp, we completed furnishing our little bush abode with some confiscated Blazo boxes.

Unalakleet was a friendly, laid-back little village. Nobody there ever seemed to worry about the time. You'd find children playing in the streets at any hour between midnight and midnight. Parents didn't worry about where their kids were, and the kids didn't worry about where their parents were. When a child got tired, he might go home, but he was just as likely to go lie down some place close at hand. The same thing was true if he got hungry; a neighbor's house was as good as home for satisfying his appetite. The people in Unalakleet just had this gentle, easygoing way of rearing their children. It was looked upon as a community responsibility.

About two days after Paul and I got into Unalakleet, a C-46 landed. The C-46 is about twice the size of the DC-3 and it created quite a stir in the village. People gathered from everywhere to watch it taxi up. The doors opened, a ramp came down and a couple of fellows started worrying a large object out of the airplane. It turned out to be a helicopter, owned by Economy Pest Control out of Yakima, Washington. The company's owner, Carl Brady, had contracted with the Coast and Geodetic Survey to provide two helicopters. The second one, on loan from Johnson Miller Flying Service in Missoula, Montana, was to arrive later that week with its pilot, a fellow named Swede Nelson. The third man in the helicopter team was a Mr. Pritchard, an absolute jewel of a mechanic.

I was standing in the crowd, watching, as Carl's Bell-47 helicopter came rolling down the ramp, when I heard an Eskimo gentleman next to me turn to his companion and say, "Boy, we sure can use that!" I couldn't figure out what he was talking about. I knew the helicopter was for the surveying work. Besides, what would the Eskimos do with a helicopter? Then I saw the reason for his confusion. On the helicopter's yellow fuselage, painted in large black letters, was the company's name, "Economy Pest Control." The Eskimo thought the government was finally going to do something about the village's biggest problem—mosquitoes.

In the spring and summer, until the first frost, mosquitoes are the dominant bird of prey in Alaska. Particularly in that country north of Anchorage, right on up to the very tip at Point Barrow. We wore hats with nets hanging down and tied around our necks to try to prevent them from getting us. And we usually wore gloves, even when the sun was out and the temperatures were high. If your clothes weren't thick enough, those mosquitoes would bore right through and tap you just like a Vermont farmer taps syrup from a maple tree.

Carl no sooner got the blades on his helicopter assembled when the weather shut down. There was nothing we could do. We all went back to our tents and waited. The wind was still blowing and the weather was still down low later that day when Commander Ellerbe tracked me down in my tent. His radio was working better than it did the year before, and he had just received an urgent message.

"Ted," he said, "there's a boy down at the mouth of the Yukon in one of the villages there who has had a gun—a twenty-two rifle—discharged into his face. They're asking if anybody could pick him up and fly him down to the hospital in Bethel. Do you think you could fly today?"

I looked out at the sky. The weather was pretty lousy. Visibility looked to be under a mile. The mouth of the Yukon was about an hour away, and it would be another two-and-a-half hours to Bethel. They wouldn't be easy flights, but I was somewhat familiar with the area, and it sounded like there was a child's life at stake here. I said I'd give it a try. However, I asked if Paul could come along to help, since the boy was very young—somewhere around six or seven.

We topped off the fuel tanks in my Cub, and, with Paul in the second seat, I headed out down the coastline, flying with the shoreline underneath the left wing and the ever-present Bering Sea off the right wing. South of Unalakleet, the land flattens out into the Yukon-Kuskokwim Delta. Over the centuries, river deposits have built it out more than 200 miles (320 km) into the Bering Sea. From the air, you can see the river channels meandering through muck. There are ponds everywhere. Occasionally you will see a little village on a high spot near a slough or along the coast. There are few hills, a couple near St. Michael and a few more near Cape Romanzof.

As we approached St. Michael, through the fog I could just make out part of the outline of the village's historic old Russian church, perched on a hilltop overlooking the sea. If the weather had been clearer, I would have also been able to see the hulks of some of the old stern-wheelers that lie at the bottom of St. Michael's harbor. In the late 1800s, the village played an important role in the great Yukon Gold Rush. Oceangoing sailing ships would bring in freight and passengers headed for the gold fields of Canada. The people and supplies would be reloaded on to stern-wheelers, which would head out of the harbor, down the Bering Sea for a few miles, then up the Yukon, for the 1,000-mile (1,600-km) trip to Dawson. On clear days, when I flew over the area that summer, I was able to pick out some of the boilers, stacks and even some of the wood from those marvelous old vessels. There were probably fifty or sixty of them on the bottom of St. Michael's Bay.

Once we passed St. Michael, the weather started to improve. When we reached the north mouth of the Yukon, we were able to see the village we were looking for. The village was split in half by this meander of the river. One side had the school and about half the town on it. On the other side was the Northern Commercial Company's Mercantile Store, where we were to pick up the boy. I was feeling a great deal of pressure to get there as soon as I could. I kept picturing this poor little fellow shot in the face; he had to be a stretcher case for sure. The sooner I could get him to the hospital, the better his chances would be.

The river was still partially frozen, especially along the shore-line. There was a big shelf of snow and ice right in front of the store. The only open area for landing was the center of the river, which looked to be around sixty- to 100-feet (18- to 30-m) wide. (Without all that snow and ice, the river was probably about 200-feet (60-m) wide.)

I landed in that fairly fast moving water, put the floats up on the shelf of snow and ice, applied the throttle and slid on up toward the store. We came up out of the river and onto the ice probably twenty feet (6 m). Everything looked pretty solid. I was sure the airplane would be fine, and taking off again wouldn't be too much of a problem. It would take a little work, but we had enough room ahead of us to drag the plane around to go back into the river for our takeoff.

Also in our favor, the weather appeared to be coming up. We could see shafts of sunlight shining down through the broken clouds. I shut down the engine and Paul and I gingerly climbed out of the airplane and hurried to the store. It was the store manager's son who had been shot.

We opened the door, prepared for the worst. Imagine our surprise when we found our little gunshot victim—the one I was certain would be a stretcher case, the one we raced here in all that lousy weather to rescue—standing next to his father, perfectly mobile, with hardly a mark on him. The only indication that the youngster had had an encounter with a twenty-two rifle was a little black mark on his cheek about the size of a big blackhead.

I looked at Paul. He just shrugged his shoulders. Oh well, emergency or not, we were there. We figured we might as well finish the job. Besides, the boy did have some lead in his cheek that probably needed to be removed.

Not trusting the weather to hold, I wanted to get going right away, but the boy was not ready. At least his father didn't think he was. Bethel was a big city and dad wanted to make sure his son was properly dressed for the trip. He sent the boy off to find a brand-new set of white work gloves. It took a little while for the lad to locate the proper size, but finally we were on our way. Well, almost.

As he was hustling the youngster out the door, Paul stopped abruptly and let out a loud whoop. "My God!" he cried. "It's heading for the Bering Sea."

I rushed out the door and looked in the direction Paul was pointing. It was the Cub. It was still sitting where I left it on that chunk of ice and snow, but the ice pan had broken off from the shore. I watched in horror as the slowly rotating ice pan hit, first one side and then the other side of the river, on its steady jog down to the sea.

Paul, the manager and I, with the young gunshot victim at our heels, ran down the river bank after the Cub. With every step, I realized that the big blocks of snow we were running on could break off at any moment. We could end up floating down the river ourselves, or worse, in that frigid arctic water. We ran down to about a half mile below where the airplane was and watched as it rotated its way along the shoreline.

When the Cub got close, I took hold of Paul's hand—he was the lighter of the two of us—and then the store manager's hand. As the Cub floated by, Paul reached out with his free hand and grabbed the wing tip. Well, that airplane just didn't want to stop. It wanted to keep on rotating with this big block of ice, all the way down to the sea. The three of us pulled as hard as we could. The airplane slid a little bit, then a little more. Paul kept holding tight. We were finally able to get the airplane off that big pan of ice and closer to us. Paul had a small piece of rope. He attached it to the wing strut. We let the airplane turn one more time so that the door would be on our side. While the store manager held the wing tip, Paul got in. Then we lifted in the little boy. Paul placed him in the baggage area behind his seat. We were pretty well in place by then, so I slid down, jumped on the float and climbed in. I got the engines started and taxied off the ice, down the river, turned and took off.

It wasn't until we were airborne that the full impact of what had almost happened really hit me. What if it had taken our little gunshot victim ten more minutes to find his gloves? Another two miles (3.2 km) and the Cub would have been gone, floating away somewhere on the Bering Sea. I sure wouldn't have wanted to have to explain that to Commander Ellerbe, and certainly not to Nat Brown.

When we finally landed in Bethel, it was obvious that the hospital staff was under the same misconception that we had been. There was a two-man emergency team with a stretcher waiting for us. We turned the boy over to them and headed back home. I found out later that the doctors were able to remove the lead from the boy's face with no difficulty and sent him home three days later on a regular Alaska Airline flight.

The weather was down to the deck on the direct route back to Unalakleet so Paul and I decided to go up the Yukon. The farther we went, the further down the weather went. It grew darker and the wind was blowing. We ended up going over a pass that took us into Unalakleet through the back door. It was hard work all the way. As we parked the plane, I thought about that trip. Paul and I had just flown seven hours in mostly marginal weather. We had just about lost our airplane. And, after all that, we didn't really end up saving anyone's life. Somehow it just didn't seem like it was worth the effort, but I'm sure the young man we took to Bethel appreciated getting all that lead out of his cheek.

Chapter 10

Settling In

In the summer of 1952, our survey area was from Unalakleet to Cape Romanzof, on the coast of the Bering Sea, and up the Yukon to a point where we tied into a grid being surveyed by another group. It was the last leg of a three-year project, and the pressure to finish was on. We began by hauling men and equipment to a lake about halfway between Unalakleet and St. Michael, where Commander Ellerbe's team was setting up a secondary base camp. As I said, the weather in the area was not particularly conducive to flying. The marine layer had a bad habit of slipping in and just hanging around. When we did get good flying weather, we would try to get in as many loads as we could.

On one day, we started out at about eight o'clock in the morning and didn't finish up until midnight. We would load up, fly for about twenty-five minutes, touch down and unload at the new camp, then turn around and head back to base camp to begin the process all over again.

To make the work go faster, Paul and I decided to operate as a team. We would help each other load and gas up, then we would take off in formation. Flying in formation was a lot of fun. Every once in a while, to break up the monotony, whoever was in the lead would try to lose the other airplane by performing a maneuver to fake him out. We never did anything that would put the other fellow in danger, of course—no quick maneuvers or anything like that. Just a good tight formation, with enough interesting moves to make the pilot in back stay alert and keep a close eye on the lead pilot.

Nothing to get us in trouble, at least, not intentionally. There was one time, however, that our formation flying got my partner, Paul, into a little predicament. It happened on that very long day I just mentioned.

On the evening of that day, Paul was flying just off my right side, his wing tip about twenty feet (6 m) from my airplane. He was back in position so that we kind of overlapped. When we flew over the campsite, I dove down and got very close to the water, maybe seventy feet (21 m) from it. I was going at a good speed, around 120 miles (192 km) an hour, with the throttle pretty well open. Paul was tucked in on my right-hand side. I pulled up and made a wing-over maneuver, then pulled the power back and started a left turn. Paul was on the outside of the turn.

As I went into the turn, I pulled the flaps for landing, because they dissipated the speed in this big climb. I put the nose down, came back around and touched down on the water close to the campsite, then pulled the mixture control. I didn't need any more thrust to get to the shoreline. The airplane—everything—was working beautifully.

When I opened my door, I noticed that I couldn't hear Paul on the water. I looked over to where he should have been. He was there all right, at an angle to me, going toward the shoreline, but he was still in the air. Paul had needed a little more energy at the top of the turn to come around the outside of me, so he added power. He hadn't realized how close we were landing to the shore.

Paul touched down, but he never came off the step. His airplane slid out of the water and rattled across the top of the rocks. I thought to myself: Oh, boy, we're going to damage a float here; we're going to bend one up real good. Paul's Cub finally came to a stop, high and dry. When he opened his door, there was a sheepish smile on his face.

"Well," he drawled, in his usual, laid-back manner. "I kind of misjudged that one."

Maybe so, but I still felt responsible. The way I landed, I did kind of sucker him into the situation.

Fortunately, the damage wasn't as bad as I had feared. Paul's unconventional landing had put only one small hole in the bottom of a float. All we had to patch it with was a piece of an empty Blazo can. We got out a pair of tin snips and a drill. After rocking the airplane up on its side and pounding the aluminum down where the rock had pierced it, we drilled a couple of holes. Using a piece of raincoat for a gasket, we bolted the Blazo-can patch onto the bottom of the float, making sure that our repair job left as smooth a surface as possible. That makeshift patch lasted the whole summer without a leak, but it took us about two-and-a-half hours to get Paul's airplane back in the air again. From that day on, you can bet we both paid more careful attention to our formation flying.

One of our challenges that summer was a little lake, or, to be more exact, a little pond, behind St. Michael. Lumber, cement, food and some other supplies for the job had been stored at an old army camp in the village. The helicopters would pick up the materials and fly them over beside this little pond. Paul and I would then take over from there.

But before we could fly the materials the eighty miles (128 km) or so to the outlying campsites, we had to get them into the Cubs. This was no easy task. The tundra between where the helicopter dropped off the materials and the edge of this little pond, where our Cubs parked, was soggy marshland, covered with heavy, wet grass. The job was slow, slippery and labor-intensive. We were grateful when some of the surveyors volunteered to help us out.

Once the plane was loaded, our next challenge was to get it into the air. We had no problem getting into the lake; there were two good approaches, one on each end. But taking off was another story. That little pond was nestled in a hillside that reached up about 200 feet (60 m) in a fairly gentle slope. Normally, we didn't take off across the lake unless the wind was blowing hard.

After a while, Paul and I developed some techniques for getting the Cubs off with as big a load as possible. We figured out how to judge the load so that with a particular wind blowing, we could make it out of the lake with about 100 feet (30 m) to spare. But you really had to fly the airplane carefully and you had to be diligent about the weight you were carrying. I learned the importance of that diligence first hand.

On this particular day we were blessed with a good wind. I had made about four takeoffs and gone up the slope with no problems. But each time I had to judge my load carefully and pay meticulous attention to my air speed and flap settings. At the end of the day, I had only a small load left to get out: about twenty gallons (91 l) of gasoline, a few two-by-fours and around thirty pounds (13.5 kg) of food. However, there was also one surveyor left who had been helping us carry the stuff from the helicopter to the airplane. It was cold, and I was sure he was hungry after all that work. I hated to leave him there just sitting around on the edge of the lake with nothing to do for an hour and a half until I could return for him. His only other option would have been to spend the night in St. Michael, but it was a long, tough hike to the village, and there was really no place comfortable for him to stay once he got there.

"What do you weigh?" I asked him. The man was wearing a big, heavy trench coat so it was hard to tell by looking at him.

"Oh, about 155 pounds," he said.

"Gosh, that seems awful light."

"Well, I'm not real big. Just kind of sinewy."

Like I said, he had this big coat on and I really hadn't paid much attention to his size, so I believed him. He got in the back of the airplane. I pushed the throttle for takeoff and set the flaps so we could get up on the step as quickly as possible. Then I let the flaps off and let the airplane accelerate. I took off toward that long-sloping hillside because the wind was blowing about fifteen miles (24 km) an hour from that direction. That made a big difference on how much space it would take to get the Cub in the air.

I could tell almost immediately that it wasn't going well. I didn't get on the step as quickly as I needed to, but things were happening pretty fast. The shoreline was coming up. I waited until the last moment, then pushed ahead on the stick with a normal short-area takeoff so that the airplane would kind of bob out of the water. Then I pulled back on the stick and at the same time pulled the flaps onto takeoff flap position. The airplane was just coming out of the water and starting to fly when I felt this big bump. The back of the floats had hit the shoreline.

All the way up the hillside, the Cub struggled on the verge of a stall. I thought: Oh, my gosh, we're going to land in the grass up here. Will that ever be embarrassing. I wasn't worried about damaging the airplane. I was thinking about how tough it was going to be to get the Cub all the way back down that hill and into the lake again. The farther up the hill we got, the more worried I became. But I didn't abort the flight. As long as we were still in the air, I decided to stick with it. We continued upward, shadowing the slant of the slope. Then, just when I was certain the plane was going to stall, we broke over the top. I was finally able to let the nose down, and we flew away.

The important lesson I learned that day was don't ever trust a fellow's estimate of his weight when you know he is anxious to get out of the area. Later, I found out that my passenger weighed thirty pounds (13.5 kg) more than he had told me—just enough extra weight to throw off my calculations and produce that hair-raising takeoff.

A little historic note about the area near the mouth of the Yukon that we were working in that summer: it had been surveyed before by the Coast and Geodetic Survey back in the late 1890s and early 1900s. In fact, we used that survey as part of the foundation for our work. The commander and his team studied their predecessors' records to locate the original markers. Frequently, the diary that the commander's team worked from would say something like "whiskey bottle placed narrow end down" in a given location. It was a real tribute to those hardy old surveyors that they were able to drink enough whiskey to leave all those markers, and still remain sufficiently sober to tell us where they were.

Those original surveyors did a truly monumental job, considering that they had to trudge, with all their gear, from the beaches where they were left off, through barely passable tundra, to climb up those hills and mounds where they placed their whiskey markers. And here we were, in 1952, doing the same thing, only in a fraction of the time with a fraction of the effort, using both fixed-winged airplanes and helicopters.

Our two helicopter pilots, Carl Brady and Swede Nelson, were as different as night and day. Carl was an intense, hardworking individual, with little time or patience for humor. He was only interested in one thing: getting in all the flying hours he could so that his company would have the biggest possible gross income at the end of the summer. Carl's commitment to hard work and his entrepreneurial talents paid off down the line. He eventually became owner and president of Era Helicopters in Anchorage. When Rowan Drilling bought him out, the deal made him the biggest stockholder in that parent company. Today, Era is one of the real powerhouse air carriers and helicopter operators in the state of Alaska. The company places airplanes and people all over the world to support the work of mining and oil companies. But, back in the fifties, Carl was sort of a one-man band. Well, perhaps two-man band, if you count the partner he left down in Yakima to look after their Economy Pest Control company. Work, as I said, was always foremost on Carl's mind.

Swede, who was on loan to Carl's company from the Johnson Brothers Flying Service, was also a hard worker, but he believed fervently in having fun in the process. He was a tall, sturdy man with a round face that crinkled up around the eyes from smiling a lot and squinting into the sun, something that can't be helped when you're a pilot. That summer, Swede grew a mustache and a full beard. With all that wild blond hair, combined with his weather-worn face and that booming, slightly wicked laugh of his, he seemed like a reincarnation of one of those legendary Viking sea captains.

Swede was a crack pilot; his skill with the helicopter was second to none. And right up there with his flying skills was his skill as a first-class prankster. This made him great fun to work with, although I have to admit that when I ended up the butt of his joke, I had to get some distance from his mischief before I could fully appreciate the humor in it. Take the time he decided to play tag with me during an embarrassingly intimate moment.

I was at the lake, waiting for Swede to fly in with another load from the warehouse in St. Michael, when nature called. Finding a suitable bush, I began to relieve myself. I had no sooner started when I heard the sound of Swede's rotors approaching. I guess seeing me standing there by that bush so vulnerable was more than he could resist. He brought his helicopter in real close and just hovered there, with his rotors churning up the wind all around me. The steady stream of liquid I was trying to expel was suddenly flying all over the place, mostly over me. I tried to stop it, but Swede moved in closer and began bumping my hip with the skid of his helicopter, which, of course, sabotaged any efforts I made to regain control of my bodily functions.

I can look back now and laugh at the situation, and certainly admire Swede's skill with his machinery. To get that close to me without hurting me was quite an accomplishment. But at the time I thought Swede's antics showed great irreverence on his part. He, on the other hand, thought his little prank was one of the funniest things he had ever done and, much to my embarrassment, wasn't the least bit shy about describing the scene to anyone who would listen.

In May, the Army Mapping Corps arrived in Unalakleet with a series of large ships. Paul and I went down to the beach to watch them unload. They were transferring their cargo to LCM6s, which are fifty-five-foot- (16.5-m-) long landing barges. A crane had just picked up a large crate from a ship's deck and was swinging it over the water toward a landing barge when one of the cables holding the crate snapped and the huge box dropped into the Bering Sea.

From all the groaning on shore, I thought for certain that the corps had just lost a critical piece of equipment, until one of the soldiers standing in the crowd threw up his hands and whined, "There goes all our private treasures." It seems that the Army Mapping Corps was anticipating some downtime while they were in Unalakleet. The box that had just been claimed by the sea was filled with guns, fishing rods and other personal items for the pursuit of pleasure on their off-hours. Obviously, their deadlines weren't quite as tight as ours.

A good example of the difference between the manner in which Commander Ellerbe's team and the Army Mapping Corps approached their work occurred a few days later. The army had brought in L-19 Bird Dog airplanes and L-20 DeHavilland Beavers, both on floats. It had also brought in a whole series of LCM6s, to carry its personnel and gear up the Yukon River (in traditional full-blown army fashion). The airplanes were lined up beside our two Cubs in that small estuary behind Unalakleet.

Paul and I were working on our Cubs when one of the pilots for the L19 Bird Dogs showed up. The Bird Dog was a Cessna, basically an observation airplane. It was about twice the horsepower of our Super Cubs, but while it could do a little bit of freight work if it cared to, it couldn't carry as big a load as a Cub. It was fun to be able to outperform these big, fancy airplanes when they moved into our arena.

Standing on the edge of the water, the L19 Bird Dog pilot looked down at his feet. He was wearing a pair of spiffy brown oxfords. I looked down at my feet and my reliable, well-worn hip boots, and smiled at Paul.

There was a mechanic working on the Bird Dog; he was a sergeant. The lieutenant called him over. I couldn't believe my ears.

The pilot actually asked the sergeant to carry him, piggyback, out to the airplane, so he wouldn't get his shoes wet. Paul and I chuckled to ourselves at the sight of the sergeant, sloshing through the water, with the lieutenant on his back. We wondered what the lieutenant was planning to do when he landed at wherever he was going. Chances of him finding another sergeant there to carry him were slim. How was he ever going to get to shore without getting his nice shoes all wet?

The Army Mapping Corps had an impressive operation at Unalakleet: a battalion of about 400 men and all that equipment— boats, airplanes, helicopters, the whole works. But because of the corps' size, not to mention its inexperience in this kind of terrain, as the summer progressed it took the group more effort to get its part of the job done than our group. Watching them taught me another important lesson: numbers and technology have their advantages, but when you are working out in the bush, it's more efficient to work lean and mean, and definitely with experienced people.

Chapter 11

Alakanuk Revisited

About the middle of the summer, Commander Ellerbe made arrangements to move our base camp from Unalakleet down to the south mouth of the Yukon River. We would be working out of the Yupik Eskimo village of Alakanuk at the east entrance of Alakanuk Slough. This, if you remember, is where John, Nat and I spent an extended refueling stop the summer before, on our way to St. Lawrence Island, and where I collected my very first "Alaska" story. One of the surveyors told me that the village was more or less "discovered" by G.R. Putnan of the U.S. Coast and Geodetic Survey, who first reported it in 1899.

The move to and the work at the new location required another aircraft, something bigger than the Cubs. The Coast and Geodetic Survey contracted with a fellow named Bud Priest, who was to meet us at Unalakleet with his Travelair 6000. I looked forward to this addition to our flying team. The Travelair carried six or seven people and had a good reputation for performance.

The day the Travelair was suppose to arrive came and went with no sign of Priest. He finally showed up a week and a half later with his wife and daughter in tow. They had no place else to go, he told us, so they were going to stay with him in his tent. I suspect he just didn't have the money to put them up anywhere else. Bud apologized for his late arrival. He said he had fallen behind schedule in getting the Travelair ready. As far as I could see, it still wasn't ready. I went to talk to Commander Ellerbe.

I told the commander that I didn't think the Travelair was safe to fly in. I had spotted some mis-riggings on cables and some other problems. The news didn't please him. Bud's late arrival had already put us a week and a half behind schedule. But, as usual, Commander Ellerbe's first consideration was for the safety of his men. "Okay," he said, "you check it out and let me know what needs to be done." I felt kind of bad, like I had turned Bud in, but he thanked me later and said I did him a service. And that was probably true. After all, he did end up with a safer airplane and the Coast and Geodetic Survey footed the bill.

When Paul and I went to check out the Travelair, we found even more problems than I had anticipated. For one thing, there was the elevator control. When you pulled it back to its full up-travel position, you ended up with the wheel only an inch from the seat. This explained Bud's flat landing the first day he flew into Unalakleet. Bud was a portly gentleman, about six feet and three inches (188 cm). There was no way that he could have pulled that wheel back far enough to get the nose up for a landing.

There were other problems. Some of the cables to the floats and the hard wires on the floats were bent or missing and needed to be replaced. We showed Bud where the problems were and, to his credit, he cheerfully fixed everything. Two days later, we relocated to Alakanuk.

If you remember, there was a cannery at Alakanuk owned and operated by the Emel family. We set up camp on part of a runway that Emel had built to service his operation. The runway didn't see much action in the summer. Most people flying into the area that time of year were on floats, including the two airlines that serviced the village: Northern Consolidated and Alaska.

One day shortly after we arrived, a Norseman, operated by Northern Consolidated, was scheduled to fly in with a new bunch of Coast and Geodetic Survey people and their equipment. The pilot was coming in for a landing right in front of the cannery, on this slough that was an offshoot of the main branch of the Yukon River. Everything appeared to be normal, but as the airplane touched down, it flipped over. Fortunately, nobody got hurt, just wet, and the equipment all came through in one piece. The only real casualty was the pilot's ego. I felt sorry for him. He was an experienced pilot with a good record, at least until that day. That big old Norseman, tethered to the shoreline, belly up on the river, was certainly a sight to behold.

Flying accidents can happen in spite of our best efforts, but there are some pilots who seem to court misfortune. As the summer wore on, I continued to have an uncomfortable feeling about the Travelair. It wasn't just Bud's indifferent attitude toward maintenance that troubled me; he had a flying style that put a real strain on his aircraft. Take, for example, the way Bud would get his airplane into the air. The Travelair had a two-position Hamilton propeller. It would operate at a relatively flat pitch for takeoff or in high pitch, low RPM for cruise, except when Bud was at the controls. On takeoff, Bud would set the stops so that the engine would put out its certified maximum horsepower, and then some. He would turn it about 200 RPM more than its rated 2,300 RPM. I would guess that he was probably getting 550 horsepower out of that 450-horsepower engine. That old engine stood up to it, but what a racket it made when it was operated that way at full throttle.

Once Bud lifted off the water, he didn't pull the throttle back. Instead, he would reach up and pull the prop pitch back. This would take all that RPM and convert it into a lot of surging horsepower, pulling the airplane ahead. Then he would reduce the throttle setting. I can't think of a worse thing to do to an engine, and Bud did it on *every* takeoff. He would get that two-bladed Hamilton Standard propeller operating at such a high RPM that I'm sure the tips of the blades were reaching the speed of sound because, at the end of the season, all the rivets that were in line with that propeller were loose in the floats, shaken loose by the noisy vibration of that engine.

Don't get me wrong, I liked Bud Priest. It was impossible not to like him. He was a good-natured fellow and a hard worker. He did everything he could to make the job go well. But you could tell by the way he abused his equipment that he lacked a real understanding of the principles of flight. Unfortunately, Bud ended up paying a high price for his laissez-faire attitude about safety. My fears about the Travelair never materialized that summer, but, three years later, while flying a group of magazine salesmen all over the state in a Twin Beechcraft, Bud spun and hit the ground about 100 miles (160 km) from McGrath. Everyone was killed. I felt bad for his family. They took the loss hard. He was a powerful and beloved presence in their lives. I wish, for their sake, Bud would have given a little more thought to safety when he flew.

We had a most unusual wake-up call in Alakanuk. It came every morning, courtesy of Swede Nelson. Swede was an early riser, getting up about twenty minutes before the rest of us. After he put on his clothes, he would step out into the fresh morning air and stroll down the line of tents to the cook tent. The walk would evidently get his system circulating, because halfway there, like clockwork, he would break wind. Then, with enviable musical prowess, he would instantly burst into song, skillfully matching the first note of his melody to the pitch of his breaking wind. That melodious, if somewhat odorous, performance would serve notice to the rest of us that it was time to get up.

I have always had a special affection for old ships. During our days in Alakanuk, I got to see many old tugs and steamers as they plied their trade up and down the Yukon. My favorite was the Nenana, a beautiful classic stern-wheeler. She was about 150-feet (45-m) long. Her crew had dubbed her "the Queen of the Yukon," a bit pretentious perhaps, given her age and state of repair. Yet, the name seemed to fit. There was something regal about the way she glided across the water as she pulled her cumbersome loads up and down the river. Looking at her graceful lines, it was easy to imagine her deck and once-elegant salon crowded with prospectors, gamblers and other adventurers in the days of the great Alaskan Gold Rush when the Nenana truly was the Queen of the Yukon. Every time I flew over her, I would drop down close and wiggle my wings in a kind of salute. The crew would always wave back.

One evening, as I was flying back to base camp after my final run of the day, I spotted the Nenana just as she was pulling into one of the little villages along the river. This time, when I circled around and wiggled my wings, the skipper stepped out of the wheelhouse and waved a cup at me—an invitation to drop in for some coffee and conversation.

Things like that happened all the time that summer. Hardly a week went by that didn't present an opportunity to make another friend and gain some new insights about the territory. I touched down, tied up behind the ship with a short piece of rope, and jumped aboard.

The captain and I sipped coffee in the wheelhouse as he told me all about the graceful stern-wheeler and about his main destination up river, the town of Nenana, after which his ship had been named.

Nenana is an Athabascan word meaning "a good place to camp between the rivers." It is certainly an appropriate name for the little community, sitting as it does on the south bank of the Tanana River, just east of the mouth of the Nenana River.

Although the discovery of gold in Fairbanks in 1902 brought intense activity to the region, Nenana would probably still be an obscure little village if it were not for a bunch of bored railroad workers back in 1917. Having run out of amusements while waiting for the spring thaw, these construction workers devised the popular Alaskan game of chance known as the "Nenana Ice Classic." And every year since, people from all over Alaska eagerly play the game, coughing up the two dollars to bet on the exact day, hour and minute that the ice on the Tanana River will break up.

It's clever how they figure it out. A four-legged tripod is set up on the river ice in February. The tripod has a cable that runs to a clock tower on the river bank. When the ice moves, the cable stops the clock, recording the official time. And whoever guesses correctly walks away with a bundle that, I believe, is now somewhere around $100,000.

I enjoyed the captain's tales about the Nenana and the little town up river, but I was more interested in the helpful tips he was able to give me on how to read the currents of the Yukon. He showed me where the river braided and what to look out for when I flew by, so that I would know where it would be safe to land. Even today, whenever I think of the Yukon, I picture that elegant old stern-wheeler gracefully gliding up the river in the sunset of her career. She's gone now, but if you ever get to Nenana, which is about sixty-five miles (104 km) southwest of Fairbanks on the George Parks Highway, you can see what she looked like. The town proudly displays a replica of her for visitors. And while you are there, you just might want to pick up a two-dollar ticket for the Nenana Ice Classic.

Flying out of our new location was a lot of fun for Paul and me; it gave us a good opportunity to sharpen our bush-flying skills. The challenges here were the sandy beaches of the Yukon and the river's turbid water. The cloudiness made it difficult to tell where the water was deep and where it was shallow. To get around this problem, Paul and I employed our knowledge of geography. If the river made a big bend, we knew that the shallow part would be on the inside of the bend and the deeper part would be on the outside, so we would land and take off on the outside of the bend. But, every once in a while, you would land and be taxiing along thinking things were going just fine when, all of a sudden, you would find yourself high and dry on a sandbar.

This happened to me one day while I was carrying a small load to a station up the Yukon. I followed my usual practice of touching down on the outside of a big bend in the river. I had just come off the step and was slowing up when my airplane suddenly lurched to a stop. There I was, with the tail of my floats in water probably forty-feet (12-m) deep and the nose of the floats in water only two-inches (5-cm) deep.

I climbed out onto the float and tried to rock the airplane back off the sandbar. The tail swung a little, but the Cub remained stuck. Deciding I could get better leverage if I stood in the river, I jumped into the water. Big mistake! The shallow river bottom was like quicksand. Every time I tried to pick one foot up, the other foot would sink farther into the sand. With every step, I buried myself deeper and deeper into the shoreline. I was by myself on this trip; there was nobody around to pull me out. The situation became scary.

Finally, after struggling for a while, I managed to pull myself up enough to lay the top of my body over the float, which enabled me to pull my feet up out of that sticky mess. Just a few feet away, I could see the water running deep and swift. Fortunately, I was only carrying a small load. I kept shifting my weight to rock the plane until I finally rocked it off that sandbar and back into deep water.

I had another sticky situation a few weeks later, but this time I was able to turn the circumstances to my advantage. This happened on the Black River, a few miles south of the south mouth of the Yukon, on the way to Cape Romanzof.

The Black River's tides are greatly influenced by the Bering Sea. In fact, they rise and fall almost identically. One day, when the tide was out, I landed in the narrow, watery portion of the river. As I turned toward shore, ahead of me I could see about thirty to forty yards (27–36 m) of very black, gooey material going all the way up to the shoreline. Getting out of the airplane, cautiously this time, I took a tentative step into this black goop and promptly sank almost up to my knee. I had to drop off the supplies I was carrying, but there was no way I could walk them across those thirty or forty yards (27–36 m) to shore, not over that soft, slippery mess. Slippery! That gave me an idea.

I got back into the airplane and started up the engine, gingerly adding power. My gamble paid off. The Cub just scooted across that slippery mud and I was able to taxi all the way up to the high tide shoreline in the grass, where I unloaded the airplane. When it came time for takeoff, I had a little luck. It started to rain, not a lot, but enough to put a slick surface on top of that goopy mud. That surface provided the fastest acceleration I have ever experienced. Before I knew it, I was on the step and taking off into the wind, a 100-foot (30-m) run at the very most.

Since I had quite a bit of freight to bring into this location, I thought I'd try landing on that slick goop again. It worked like a charm. The airplane just slid right in. I slithered up to where I wanted to unload the freight, threw it off on the grass and took off again. Paul came out and saw the operation. It looked good to him, so he tried it with equal success.

If you fly in the bush any length of time, you are bound to come across situations your experience hasn't prepared you for, like that slick, soft mud; situations that force you to use your wits or rely on your gut instincts. That's the creative part of bush flying, the part that makes it fun. Sometimes you get into a situation and come up with an idea that your common sense tells you will never work, but the temptation to try it is so strong that you can't resist. That, too, is a part of the fun of bush flying.

I was on my way back to camp after picking up some materials from the Army Mapping Corps in Unalakleet. As I passed over some hills just north of the north mouth of the Yukon River, I happened to look down. This one hill had a little lake on it, and leading off from the lake and up the hill (or down the hill into the lake—it was hard to tell which) were these mysterious tracks about the length of a football field. The funny thing about them was that they were darker down by the lake and lighter the farther they got from the lake. They looked a lot like seaplane tracks, but that didn't make any sense. Seaplanes just don't go up or down hills like that. And where, I wondered, was whatever had made those tracks now? Not at the bottom of the lake, I hoped. I pondered the mystery the rest of the way back to camp.

Dinner was just about over by the time I touched down and

made my way to the cook tent. I grabbed my food and joined Paul and a surveyor from South Carolina named Earl, who were just finishing up.

"You wouldn't believe what's out there on that slope up there by the north mouth," I told them as I sat down. When I began to describe what I saw, they both laughed.

"What's so funny?"

"I did it," Paul said. "I made those tracks." And he told me the following story.

Paul had taken Earl out to that hill to do some survey work. He had two possibilities for landing: the Bering Sea and that little lake about two-thirds of the way up the hill. Considering how small the lake was, it would have been easier, and probably more prudent, to land and take off from the Bering Sea. However, the lake was closer to the survey site, which meant less hiking. Therefore, it was, naturally, Earl's preference.

"Oh, come on," he goaded Paul, "you can land on that lake." Paul dropped down and did a flyover to measure it. It was small, but the wind was blowing at about fifteen to twenty miles (24–32 km) an hour. With that much wind, Paul figured that he could touch down and get off easy enough, so he came back in and landed.

The two men hiked up to the top of the hill, where they found the whiskey bottle that had been placed there sixty years before. They put in a new marker and a set of the white banners that we were using to identify the locations for aerial photography, and hiked back down to the airplane. Just about then, the wind quit.

"This lake is too small to take off from without some wind," Paul told Earl as they climbed into the Cub. "We're going to have to wait until it starts blowing again."

"Oh, come on, Paul, you can make it," Earl urged.

Against his better judgment, possibly because he was as anxious as Earl was to get back to camp, Paul decided to give it a try. He opened the throttle and got up on the step, but the Cub hit the shoreline before he could get it into the air. Paul pulled the power off immediately. It still took the two of them a good hour to get the airplane back down the hill and into the water again.

Paul taxied back across the lake and pulled up on the other shoreline. The two men took out their ever-present books and read while they waited for the wind to return. After a while, Earl grew restless. The air was still dead calm; there was no sign that the wind would be coming up any time soon. He tapped Paul on the shoulder. "What would happen if you started up and got it going on that grass on the other side? Wouldn't this thing fly?"

"I don't think so," Paul said. "I really don't know."

"Well, let's give it a try. If we don't get out of here soon, we're not going to get back in time for dinner, maybe not even for breakfast."

Don't ask me how Earl talked the usually cautious Paul into it. Or maybe he didn't talk him into it. Maybe the idea was so intriguing that Paul couldn't resist trying it. In any case, he opened the throttle and off they went across the lake. They bounced up onto the grass and kept on bouncing, farther and farther from the lake, until (I still find it hard to believe) they bounced right into the air.

As Paul was telling the story, I thought about my own experience earlier in the season, when I bumped the lip of a lake as I attempted a takeoff up a hill with too heavy a load. I skimmed the hillside, but at least I was in the air. I wasn't trying to ride my pontoons up that slope like a pair of wheels, or more accurately, pogo sticks. By all logic, Paul's little gamble shouldn't have paid off, but for some reason, it did. I'll tell you one thing: neither Paul nor I had any desire to test this novel takeoff technique a second time.

While I was in Unalakleet picking up some materials from the Army Mapping Corps, I ran into an old friend from my previous summer on St. Lawrence Island: the helicopter pilot from Kern Copters that we all called Black Bart. Bart was in Unalakleet to help fulfill a contract Kern had with the Corps to provide civilian helicopters for its project that summer. Like me, he had discovered that this area of Alaska presented pilots with a whole different set of challenges than the ones we faced on St. Lawrence Island. For him, the biggest challenge was the region's preponderance of soft ground.

The 47G that Bart was flying had skids for landing gear. Because the helicopter had more weight toward the back of the skids than the front, when Bart would set down on soft ground and turn off the main rotor blade, the combination of the loss of lift and the weight of the tail would cause the skids to sink down until the stinger, or sometimes even the tail rotor blade, touched the turf.

The Kern mechanic had a fix for the problem. He fitted triangular boards flat-wise, two of them, on the heel of the skids, so that when a pilot touched down on soft ground, there would be more flotation to hold the helicopter up. But, as Bart was well aware, it was far from a perfect fix. That's why he was always careful about easing the lift off the main rotor blade. That way, if he saw he was going to settle in, he could pick back up and find better ground. Finding better ground was exactly what Bart was trying to do the day he mystified the natives of a little Eskimo village on the Yukon River close to St. Mary's Mission.

Paul and I just happened to be in the village that day when Bart was coming in for a landing. The villagers had never seen a helicopter before. Everyone rushed out to watch. In his effort to find some solid ground to set down on, Bart hovered about a foot and a half in the air, turning in a tight little circle, while he leaned out and studied the ground below. He kept going around and around as the puzzled villagers watched. Finally, one of the Eskimos turned to Paul and me and said with conviction, "Stuck!" His companions nodded their heads in agreement. They thought the helicopter was stuck in the air and couldn't land. Paul and I found the idea pretty funny, but I guess to someone who had never seen a helicopter before, that's exactly what Bart's maneuver looked like.

Remember that "fix" the Kern Copter mechanic came up with to prevent the helicopter skids from sinking in soft ground? Well, it not only didn't solve the problem very well; it ended up costing the company a helicopter. It happened on a slow work day late in the season. With nothing to do, Bart and a friend decided to pay a visit to some surveyors Bart had befriended the year before. He set his helicopter down at their camp and he and his passenger joined the surveyors in their tent for a cup of coffee and a little conversation.

When it came time to leave, the wind had kicked up and it was raining, so the two surveyors said their good-byes indoors. After Bart and his friend left, the surveyors tied up the flap on their tent and went back to reading their pocketbooks.

Bart fired up his helicopter. He got it all warmed up and added plenty of power, but every time he tried to lift off, the nose of the helicopter would go up in the air. It seems those triangular pieces of plywood the mechanic had put on the skids for flotation were caught under a couple of clumps of grass. When Bart couldn't get the helicopter to go straight up, he tried to push forward, figuring he could lift off by picking up the back of the helicopter. That didn't work either. He applied even more power and pushed farther forward on the stick.

To understand what happened next, you need to know something about how this helicopter was put together. The engine stood vertically on the helicopter with a shaft going straight up to the main rotor and the gear box, back to the tail rotor. The way the engine and the airframe were hooked together, all the weight and the engine mount itself were at shoulder height. To keep the engine from swinging in the mount, it was secured by a double cable that went across the bottom of the engine to the air frame.

As I was saying, unable to get a normal liftoff, Bart pushed forward hard on the stick, applying plenty of horsepower ... and that crucial double cable that was holding everything together broke. Suddenly, the rotor blade, which was made of wood and plastic, dipped down. One blade touched the ground in front of the helicopter, then bounced back up and hit the tail boom, tearing it right off. The blade broke up, sending splinters of wood everywhere. Almost simultaneously, the next blade came around, smashed into the ground and put more splinters of wood all around the helicopter. Then the engine tore out of the air frame and the whole thing came apart.

It was at that instant that the two surveyors, hearing the commotion outside, opened up the flap of their tent to see what was going on. What they saw was Bart and his passenger, still sitting in their seats, with their helicopter completely gone. And surrounding them were all the splintered pieces of the main rotor, stuck in the ground and pointing back at them like a bunch of swords. It didn't take the two surveyors long to appreciate their own narrow escape. Had they been outside to watch the helicopter's departure, as they normally would have been if it hadn't been windy and raining, there is no doubt that they would have been impaled by one of those deadly splinters. Luckily, neither Bart nor his passenger suffered any injuries in the mishap, but they were left with no transportation home. Another helicopter had to be sent out to rescue them.

Chapter 12

Getting Even and Flying Backward

I guess you are either born with a sense of humor, or you're not. If you aren't, there's not much anyone can do to make you see the fun in something. That's the lesson I learned one bright, sunny day when Paul and me, in our Cubs, and Swede and Carl, in their helicopters, made a trip down the coast to Scammon Bay, near Cape Romanzof. The plan was for Paul and me to transfer our loads to Swede and Carl when we got to the bay. They would then carry the double loads up to the top of a mountain on the cape.

The helicopters took off a few minutes before we did, but they were slower. I could see them flying along behind us in the bright sunlight. Now, I hadn't forgotten about the little trick Swede had played on me earlier that summer when he unceremoniously interrupted my efforts to "relieve myself." It occurred to me that this might be a good time to pay him back.

Carl was on the right in the Economy Pest Control helicopter; Swede was on the left in the Johnson Brothers' 47G. I circled around and approached Swede from his left side, at about his same altitude, but a full two airplane-lengths away. That way, if Swede decided to make a turn, for example, we wouldn't tangle. That would have been hard on my airplane, and even harder on his helicopter. I was just out to give him a little scare, not put either of us in any danger.

To create that scare, I whizzed by Swede at about twice his speed and pulled up in a wingover. He slowed down his helicopter and moved over by a bush that was sticking up, maybe ten-feet (3-m) high. I followed him. He turned around the bush and began to play hide-and-seek with me. After a couple of passes, I left, laughing. I knew my little shenanigans hadn't really scared Swede, but I had had my fun. We were even.

"Did you see me hide behind that bush?" Swede asked as soon as he landed, grinning from ear to ear. "You bet," I said. "You sure made a hard target." And we both had a good laugh.

Unfortunately, Carl did not see the humor in my little prank. As soon as Swede and I began laughing, he started yelling—accusing me of flying too close to the helicopter and endangering Swede's life and machine. I tried to explain to him that there was never any danger, not at the distance I carefully kept between us, but he wouldn't listen. Not to me, not to Swede.

After he finished chewing me out, Carl didn't speak to me again for the rest of that summer, not even to say hello. At first I chalked his reaction up to bush fever. We were all getting a little bushy by that time. But the fact is, it took Carl seven years (from 1952 to 1959) to forget about that little incident and finally forgive me enough to hold a civil conversation with me.

Carl's lack of a sense of humor obviously didn't prevent him from building a successful business in Alaska, but I still believe if you want to work or live in Alaska, a good sense of humor comes in mighty handy. It can be a kind of sanity safety net, a survival tool for coping with the harshness of the environment and the isolation you can feel out there in the bush, or even in the little villages. I think that's why Alaskans love to play pranks on each other and weave those outrageous tall tales they are known for. I witnessed the birth of one of those tall tales while I was flying out of Alakanuk that summer.

Hamilton is a little river village a few miles from the mouth of the Yukon. It wasn't very big back in 1952, but it had a Northern Commercial Mercantile (NCM) store that took care of a number of little villages in the vicinity. Like most NCM stores, this one had a HAM radio that the store owner used to communicate with the other villages up and down the coastline and along the river. Every morning and evening, there was a standard, half-an-hour call-up time during which messages were sent and received. These messages would often be about someone moving from one village to another: reports on their progress, who had just seen them, things like that.

Around the end of July, while we were putting up a survey tower in Hamilton, a series of messages came in that perturbed George, the town's NCM store operator. For almost two weeks, radio operators along the Yukon had been reporting seeing someone rowing an inflatable yellow boat down the river with a load of dynamite for George in Hamilton. The life raft–type boat was spotted at Glenow, which is not too far from Fairbanks. Pretty soon the fellow was spotted passing by Ruby, and so on.

Now you could row a load of dynamite down the river. It would be possible. But it was not likely that someone would choose to transport such an unstable cargo in that manner. Certainly George wasn't expecting any such shipment. So every time a message reporting the progress of this "man rowing a life raft full of dynamite" was received, people in town just laughed. Everyone assumed it was a prank, another tall tale in the making.

At first, George laughed, too. But after two weeks, when the reports kept coming in, he began to get more and more irritated. "All right, folks," he told them, "enough is enough. You can kid me for a while, but to get this story rolling down the entire river is too much."

George never did see the fellow who had the load of dynamite. The joke would probably have been forgotten, except for one thing. A little yellow rubber boat loaded with dynamite finally did show up out in the Bering Sea. It was spotted by a pilot named Tosh. Tosh was flying a Grumman Goose back to Nome after servicing the Morris-Knudsen camp down at Cape Romanzof when he spotted this little yellow, inflatable boat somewhere near the mouth of the Yukon. He landed the Goose and taxied up to the life raft. According to Tosh, there was this fellow in the raft, with a set of oars and a couple of boxes of dynamite.

"Where are you going?" Tosh asked the gentleman.

"Oh, I'm going to Hamilton with a load of dynamite for George," the man replied.

Tosh told him to climb into his Grumman Goose. He said that he would take him to Nome, where they'd tell somebody to come out and retrieve that load of dynamite for George. Well, the story goes that Tosh had quite an argument with the fellow. However, the man finally got up out of his seat and climbed into the Grumman Goose, and he and Tosh flew off to Nome. They left the raft with the dynamite floating around in the Bering Sea until the next storm came, at which time it probably sunk to the bottom. So, evidently, what George thought was a tall tale concocted to kid him turned out to be the real thing. Or did it? I guess only Tosh really knows for sure.

One of the exciting things about flying in Alaska is that you can have some unique experiences. Experiences, for example, like flying backward. One day, during a hard blow that had grounded the Cubs, Swede took off in his helicopter on a mission of mercy to service one of the survey camps. The camp, about thirty miles (48 km) up the Yukon from Alakanuk, was out of both fuel and food. Swede left in the morning and was expected back no later than noon. When he hadn't returned by lunchtime, Commander Ellerbe tracked me down in the mess tent.

"Ted, do you think you can fly in this wind?"

"Probably," I told him, with more conviction than I really felt.

"Well," he said, "would you go out and see if you can find Swede? I just want to make sure nothing has happened to him."

I wolfed down the rest of my lunch and, with Paul and Bud in tow, headed for my Super Cub. Both my Cub and Paul's Cub were tied to the shore on the edge of this little horseshoe lake on the back side of the camp. The lake was actually a cutoff meander of the Yukon, with willows on both sides some ten- to fifteen-feet (3- to 4.5-m) high. The wind at the time was blowing straight across the lake at about fifty knots, right at my airplane.

"Here's how I think I'm going to do this," I told my companions. "I want one of you fellows to hold onto the wing tip. You hold on as long as you can, and I'll take off into the wind, or as close to into the wind as I can. Just make sure my wing doesn't get picked up before I have control over it."

Bud was the logical one to hang on to the wing tip. He was a big man, weighing in at roughly 280 pounds (126 kg). I got into the Cub and warmed her up pretty good. Then, while Bud held on to the right wing tip, I eased off on the power. The airplane started to blow back at a little bit of an angle to the shoreline. I had the takeoff flaps on, so I just opened the throttle and flew right out of Bud's hands.

The Cub went up into the air all right, about 100 feet (30 m).

But then it just hovered there. I looked down at my controls. I was doing about sixty-five miles (104 km) an hour in air speed, but my ground speed was zero. It must have been quite a sight, because all of the fellows in camp came out to see this hovering Super Cub. Then I backed off the power just a little bit. All of a sudden, I found myself going backward. None of us had ever seen an airborne Super Cub back up before.

Actually, it doesn't matter what an airplane's speed is over the ground because it does its flying in the air. So if the air is moving at sixty-five miles (104 km) an hour, and the airplane is going sixty-five miles (104 km) an hour, the plane is still going sixty-five miles (104 km) an hour, even if the airplane's speed relative to the ground is zero.

Finally, I got the Cub moving forward. I knew it was going to take every bit of energy and skill I could muster to negotiate the weather, but I certainly didn't anticipate what happened next.

When I took off , my visibility was barely two miles (3.2 km), and the Yukon, at this point near Alakanuk, is roughly five miles (8 km) across. I added power and flew into the wind for a bit, then turned and went up river. As soon as I made my turn, my ground speed jumped from less than ten miles (16 km) an hour to about 120 miles (192 km) an hour. My instruments, of course, still indicated an air speed of sixty-five miles (104 km) an hour. The weirdest part of the experience, however, was the clouds. I knew they were moving along at the same speed as the wind, but because of their proximity to the ground, they appeared to be racing past me at high speed. It was a *very* strange sensation.

Looking down, I could see great waves on the Yukon. The current was coming down river and the wind was going up river, so the waves just stood right up, straight. Obviously, if I got into trouble, there would be no chance of landing in the river. The thing to do would be to turn into the wind and set down in the trees or in a small pond—something I hoped I wouldn't have to do.

As I continued up the Yukon, turning back and forth, carefully following the shoreline, my visibility fortunately began to improve. The wind, however, was still blasting away at me, now at somewhere around seventy miles (112 km) an hour.

About twenty minutes into the flight, I figured that I had to be fairly close to the camp Swede had gone to. However, as I looked back into the sunshine, slightly to my right, on the other side of the river, I spotted a good-sized village that I had never seen before. I couldn't understand it. It had to be an apparition. I had been flying in that part of the country for two months. I knew there were no big towns on the south side of the river. But there it was, right in front of me. I decided to take a closer look.

I couldn't believe my eyes. It was Alakanuk! The place I had just left. I had gone up the river so fast that, as I turned back and forth trying to follow the shoreline, somehow I must have gotten turned around and blown to the other side, and ended up right back where I started.

Fortunately, the improved visibility enabled me to make my discovery before I got close enough to town for anyone to see me. My little navigational error would remain my secret. I could just imagine the ribbing I would have had to take from Swede if he had ever found out.

Quickly, I picked up the shoreline again and this time managed to follow it in the right direction. After another fifteen minutes, I spotted Swede's helicopter on the ground, next to the surveyors' tent. Everything looked okay.

The Yukon River was still all stirred up, with waves running four- to five-feet (1.2- to 1.5-m) high, but I spotted a little pond about a mile behind the camp. I checked it out. It looked okay, so I buzzed the camp. When Swede came out of the tent with the surveyors, I wiggled my wings and pointed at the lake. He nodded his head, got into the helicopter and started it up. All I had to do now was figure out how to land.

The lake was big enough and somewhat sheltered by trees, but I could still see wave patterns on the water. To complicate the situation, those sheltering trees were close to thirty-feet (9-m) tall, which would make my descent a bit trickier, but I was sure I could make it. When I saw Swede lift off, I came over the trees and lined up to land into the wind.

I slowed up to keep my ground speed down and descended at about sixty miles (96 km) an hour through some pretty turbulent air. I had been told by a well-meaning mentor that the air never goes into the water, but always bounces off it, so I wasn't expecting any downdraft problems. Unfortunately, my information was wrong.

As I made my descent, the airplane pitched and rolled and

bounced. When I got down close to the water—probably about twenty feet (6 m) in the air—I got turned completely up on my side, a ninety-degree twist. There I was, looking down at my wing, just off the water, with a whirlpool dancing around the tip. I was about to hit the water sideways, which would have been the end of my Cub. Instinctively, I opened the throttle wide, pushed the stick to the opposite direction and pulled back. Luck must have been with me because the plane began to climb.

By the time I turned back around, Swede had already landed fairly close to the edge of the lake. I climbed up to about 200 feet (60 m), dusted off my feathers, primed myself a touch, and came back around to land. I don't think I ran twenty feet (6 m) on the water. I touched down almost vertically. Now my problem was how to get over to Swede.

The lake had many willows tangled about. They were around a foot above the water and about another foot under water, all tangled together. It was a tough little shoreline of leaves and bushes and limbs. I taxied over close to where Swede was—maybe thirty feet (9 m) away. There was no way I could tie up to the shore because every time I pulled the throttle back, the airplane would float backward in the lake. So I jammed the nose of the floats into the bushes and added power until the airplane pushed on through the bushes and up on top of them. I could feel the step of the float catching in the limbs. Leaving the motor running, I pulled the power all the way back. That little rascal just sat there in the bushes.

I climbed out on the float and took out the rear seat cushion, the one that stands vertically. It had a stiff tubing frame. I set it down in the front seat and pushed it all the way forward so it held the control stick forward. This lifted the tail up so that any gusts of wind that came along would force the airplane to nose down rather than lift off. Then I tied the seat belt around the stick to hold it in place, both left and right, and against the seat cushion. After securing my airplane, I stepped gingerly off into the water, which was about a foot deep (thank goodness for hip boots), and stood back for a moment, watching the Cub, to make sure it wasn't going anywhere. Luckily, it just sat there and quivered.

I sloshed my way over to Swede. He was still sitting in his helicopter with his engine running, to keep the blades from flopping. Between the sound of the Cub's and the helicopter's engines, I had to get close to hear him, so I stuck my head in his double bubble cockpit. After making some jokes about my "air show" landing performance, Swede told me why he hadn't returned to base. When he had tried to head back, he found that he was barely able to make ground speed. Afraid that he would run out of gas, he decided to wait out the weather at the surveyors' camp. After my own experiences that afternoon, I certainly understood Swede's concern. I offered him the ten extra gallons (45 l) of gas I was carrying, but he shook his head.

"I'll tell you what," he said. "I'll try to fly back to camp, if you follow me. If it turns out that we can't make any progress, we can always go over and land beside one of those lakes or come back here. If I get low on gas on our way back, then we'll put your gas in."

It sounded like a good plan to me. I headed back to the Cub, unfastened the seat belt, returned the cushion to the rear seat and, holding the stick forward, climbed in. But as I put on my seat belt and shut the door, another problem suddenly confronted me: how was I going to get my Cub back in the air? Normally, to take off, I would have just blown back into the lake. But I couldn't. Those tree limbs and roots that I had jammed my floats into to secure my Cub now held me fast. I was stuck.

Then I remembered a little trick Paul had pulled earlier that summer when he had been in a similar situation. Since he couldn't blow back into the water, he took off across the grass. Fortunately for me, I had a good, strong wind to work with, and I was sure it wouldn't take much to fly. So I put on my takeoff flaps and opened the throttle. The airplane moved ahead a little bit, then, sure enough, before I knew it, I was in the air.

As planned, I followed Swede back toward Alakanuk. There were a few times along the way that we actually didn't make any progress over the ground. But then Swede would take a little sashay to the side, or increase his power, and we would start making headway again. It was a grueling trip. Thankfully, we were able to make it back without having to land to refuel the helicopter.

We arrived at camp just in time for supper. Swede had no trouble landing in his normal spot. My landing proved to be a little trickier. As I approached the little fish-hook-shaped lake, I saw Paul and Bud waiting for me with some ropes. They must have heard me coming. As soon as I reached the shore, they used some of their ropes to hold the nose of the floats up against the shoreline and some to hold the floats down, so the airplane wouldn't tip over backward with the gusts. I climbed out and we tied the plane down as securely as we could, using some extra stakes. Then we put two-by-fours on the top of the wings to break the lift, and tied all the controls as tightly as we could. Given the fierceness of the wind that day, I was glad to see that all of our tents were still in place when we got back to camp. None of them had blown away, but it had been a wild afternoon.

During supper, Swede and I had a great time recounting our adventure to Paul and some of the surveyors. When I finished explaining how I took off from the lake, Swede turned to us and said, "You know, I finally understand why you fellows are called bush pilots. You really do fly out of the bushes."

Chapter 13

One Last Adventure

During that second summer, Commander Ellerbe and his team surveyed about 200 miles (320 km) of that flat Yukon Delta, setting up and taking down their six Bilby steel towers twenty times to get the job done. The towers got their name from Chief Signalman Jasper S. Bilby. In 1927, Bilby, concerned with costs and occasional shortages of adequate wood on site, came up with the idea of replacing the traditional wood towers the Coast and Geodetic Survey had used for their triangulations over the past 130 years with reusable prefabricated portable steel towers. The Aeromotor Corporation, a windmill manufacturer, helped him with the design.

Like their wood predecessors, the steel towers were actually two towers in one. The inner tower held the theodolite, and the outer tower, the surveyors. This way, the measuring instrument was not disturbed by the observer, assuring the greatest possible accuracy. These venerable structures graced our countryside wherever the Coast and Geodetic Survey was at work for more than sixty years, until the advent of the Global Positioning System made them, and the great triangulation parties, obsolete. The tallest of these towers was 150 feet (45 m) from ground to top. The ones we were using in Alaska were ninety feet (27 m). Of course, these double towers meant that Paul and I ended up hauling a lot of steel that summer.

Usually you can fly a Cub with almost anything that you can get in it or on it, but not in this case. It may not have looked like we were carrying much weight when we were all loaded up, but the steel in those Bilby towers was close to two-inches (5-cm) thick and extremely heavy. Paul and I had to figure the weight of our loads very carefully. We gauged how much we could carry by how far down in the water our floats went. Once loaded up, we would fly the steel out, put it up on the beach, and go back and get some more. When we had gotten about half the steel in place, we would fly in the three-man building crew. For one ninety-foot (27-m) double tower, it took about seven or eight trips.

Between hauling all that steel and the other challenges that cropped up that summer, I did some of the most intensive flying I've ever done. The first month, Paul and I put in about 120 flying hours in just twenty-five days. The next month we got in about 110 hours. The third month, August, we had well over 115 hours. By the time September came around, we were both pretty tired.

Finally, the job ended. All the men and equipment were brought back to the main camp, and loaded aboard the Nenana for what I believe was her last voyage. The old steamer carried her cargo up the Yukon to the town of Nenana, where men and equipment were transferred to rail for the journey home.

As Paul and I were packing up to leave, Commander Ellerbe sent for us. He thanked Paul for the good job he had done and then turned to me. "Ted," he said, looking me straight in the eye, "you've done everything we've asked you to do, and done it well. I appreciate it." As he shook my hand, I thought about the previous summer, when I first showed up at the camp on St. Lawrence Island, a twenty-year-old kid with no bush experience. I remembered how leery the commander was about letting his men fly with me. Fortunately for me, John Ellerbe was a fair man; he had been at least willing to give me a chance. That is something I will always be grateful to him for.

As we left Commander Ellerbe's tent, Paul let out an ear-piercing "Whoopee!" His outburst caught me by surprise; it was so out of character.

"Come on, kid, hurry up," he announced. "It's time to go to *McGrath!*"

I remember thinking at the time that he put a strange emphasis on the word "McGrath," as if going there, not going home, was what was important. But I didn't say anything. I was distracted by the weather. It was really lousy—enough rain and heavy winds to make any sensible pilot stay put. I suggested that perhaps we ought to hang around camp a little while, until we had some better flying weather. Paul brushed my concerns aside. "Don't worry," he assured me, "we'll get up the river a little ways, and the weather will get better." I wasn't convinced, but I didn't want to make the trip alone, so we loaded the Cubs, gassed up, threw in a couple extra five-gallon (23-l) cans for insurance, and headed out for McGrath.

Our first refueling spot was Marshall, about 175 miles (280 km) up the Yukon, maybe two hours of flying time. The weather never got any better. Visibility remained at about two miles (3.2 km), and the rain and wind continued to pummel our airplanes.

There were some nice folks in Marshall that summer, including a pretty half-native girl that Paul thought was very attractive, and I thought was more than very attractive. We found out that the weather ahead was all closed in. I suggested that we spend the night, but Paul was determined to push on. I had never known him to push the weather like this.

"All right, Paul," I said, "what is this all about? Why are you pushing so hard to get to McGrath?" He gave me a sheepish grin. "It's Valerie," he said, referring to Nat Brown's niece. "We've been writing to each other all summer, and she told me that she would be waiting for me in McGrath, and that she was looking forward to seeing me."

I realized then that I was dealing here with a man hopelessly in love. There was no use trying to talk any sense into him. The only thing on Paul's mind was getting to Valerie as quickly as possible. So we gassed up again and headed out. To try to find some better weather, we decided to fly across the flats between the Yukon and the Kuskokwim, to Sleetmute. We arrived there right at dusk.

If we had gassed up in any other place, I think I would have pushed to spend the night there, given the weather we were dealing with and the time of day. But, in those days, Sleetmute wasn't exactly a village you would want to spend the night in. It had no facilities, which meant that we would have had to stay with a private family. Ordinarily that would be no problem. Most Alaskan villages were friendly, peaceful places. But Sleetmute had a reputation for being a rough, hard-drinking, violent town, so I didn't put up much of an argument when, after we each took on about fifteen gallons (68 l) of gas, Paul wanted to take off again. However, I told him that I really needed to get some lights on my Cub first.

"Don't worry about it, kid. I've got lights on my Cub," he said. "You just fly in formation with me, and we will be in McGrath in no time. It will be an easy trip." As I said, Paul wasn't interested in anything that would slow him down and keep him away from Valerie one moment longer than necessary.

While the Kuskokwim River cuts a pretty broad valley through the hills between McGrath and Sleetmute, at night, with tall trees on both sides of the river, no guiding lights and poor visibility, it didn't look like a very good operation to me. However, I sure didn't want to stay in Sleetmute by myself. Reluctantly, I agreed to forgo the lights.

We took off up river, toward McGrath. I was droning along in the mist and the rain, following Paul's lights, when suddenly they weren't there. Paul's Cub just disappeared. I looked all around, but he was nowhere in sight. Without a radio, there was no way I could talk to him.

Fortunately, I could see a sort of a glimmer here and there on the water below, so I could tell where I was. But there wasn't very much light because of the overcast and the position of the sun at sunset. It was all pretty spooky. I kept looking out for Paul, hoping I wouldn't bump into him—or that he wouldn't bump into me.

With each passing moment, I could feel the muscles in my neck grow tighter. I had taken my share of chances in bad weather over the summer, but always for a good reason: to look for a missing pilot or help someone in trouble. It was sheer lunacy for me to be flying without lights in this weather, at this time of day, risking my life, for the sake of romance. But then, I was just twenty years old. I didn't know yet what it was like to be in love. All I knew was that I was cold, tired and, while I hated to admit it to myself, scared.

I flew by a trapper's cabin on the north side of the river. He must have heard me coming because he stepped out on his porch and waved a lantern at me. I would have liked to have taken him up on his invitation, but I wasn't about to chance a landing in the river. Not without knowing where the sandbars or the rock bars were, how fast the river was moving, or what the shoreline was like. So I pushed on to McGrath, hugging the river, and keeping a constant wary eye out for Paul.

Finally, I saw McGrath up ahead. I was preparing to land on the river when I looked over at the runway. What I saw sent a chill up my spine. Although I could barely make them out, the green and white tower lights set up for the airlines were rotating, indicating normal landing conditions. But the circle of lights around the tetrahedron or wind tee—the large T-shaped weather vane that shows pilots wind direction—was blinking. Blinking lights indicate a situation below instrument-flying conditions. That meant that I was about to land on a river I couldn't see, in conditions that weren't good enough to bring a commercial airliner into the McGrath airport using instruments. But I had no choice.

I set myself up to land in the bend of the river across from the top of the "T" of the airport runway, a spot I was familiar with from my last visit. Since I couldn't see the water, I slowed my speed for a gentle descent. Down I went ... and down and down. It seemed to me that it was a lot farther down to the water than I had remembered.

I finally touched down, making a gentle turn toward the runway, off to my right. The river current was strong, but I had expected it to be. It was always strong there in McGrath. What I hadn't expected was how low the river was—a good twenty feet (6 m) lower than during my last visit in the spring. At that time, between the rains and spring runoff , the river reached deep into the bend by the "T" in the airport runway—the spot I had been aiming for. But, now, it was filled with gravel. A chilling thought crossed my mind: if I had come down just a few feet deeper into that curve, instead of landing on water, I would have shredded my pontoons on that gravel.

I looked around. Paul's Cub was nowhere in sight. I climbed out of the airplane. The green scrub willows on the edge of the river that we normally tied up to were at least fifty yards (46 m) away. I didn't have enough rope to reach them, so I built a cairn of rocks to tie the floats to. The whole time I kept thinking about Paul. I was worried that something had happened to him. But it would have been futile and foolish to try to go back out there in the dark to look for him.

With a heavy heart, I pulled my sleeping and duffle bags out of the back of the Cub and started for the runway and the roadhouse beyond. Just then I heard a plane taxiing toward me in the water. I waited a few minutes. Paul turned on his landing light and pulled up on the gravel.

I couldn't believe it. I had pushed about as hard as I had ever pushed and, quite frankly, had never been more terrified during a flight in my life. And there was Paul, emerging from his plane, all smiles, as if he had just completed another routine flight. I was furious, and determined to let him know exactly how I felt. Before I could get the words out, Paul lifted his hand and stopped me.

"Yeah, yeah, but we're here, and in a few minutes I'll get to see Valerie. So just be a good fellow and carry these over to the roadhouse for me," he said, handing me his bags. "I'll see you at Jack McGuire's." Before I could respond, he disappeared into the night, whistling as he went.

Still fuming, and now burdened down with a double load, I staggered across the runway. The roadhouse had one main sleeping room up in the loft for about twenty pilots. Yes, the lady said, there was room for two more. I think the price was fifteen dollars apiece. I climbed the stairs, dumped our gear down on two empty bunks, and headed for Jack McGuire's Bar.

As I said, the weather had been lousy all day. No pilot in his right mind would have ventured into the air unless he had to, so it was no surprise that the establishment was nearly deserted. I found Paul seated at the bar. He had a glass of whiskey in his hand and a forlorn look on his face that instantly defused my anger. It didn't take a genius to figure out that something had gone very wrong with the poor fellow's dream of romance.

"She left," he told me. "Yesterday, for Seattle, with another pilot."

I couldn't believe it. We had just risked our lives so Paul could see the lady again, and she had left the day before, without so much as leaving him a note. I gave Paul some time to sufficiently drown his disappointment, then guided my unsteady partner back to the roadhouse so we could both get some much-needed sleep.

The next day, Paul and I gave Nat Brown a hand getting his airplanes up out of the Kuskokwim. Valerie's name never came up. In the daylight, the change in the river was even more dramatic. The once-broad, fast-flowing river was now a narrow stream about one-third its springtime size.

We loaded the airplanes onto a big flat trailer and, pulling the trailer with a jeep, hauled them up, off the gravel, onto the runway and over to the airplane storage area. When we were done, Nat gave us our checks, and me my airline ticket. I thanked him for keeping his word in every way. He shook my hand and said he appreciated that I hadn't bent his airplane and was so diligent about the 100-hour inspections. Not all his pilots returned their planes in such good shape, he said.

Nat was a fascinating character. Before going to Alaska, he was one of the real trailblazers for Pan American World Airways in South America. He helped fly the Andes and all the back country of that continent. Bob Reeve, another Alaskan bush pioneer, was in South America about the same time. They both moved to Alaska within a year of each other—Nat going out into the Bethel area, and Bob starting out in the Valdez region. Along with Noel Wein and Joe Crossan, they were real pioneers of Alaskan bush flying, and I enjoyed the few tales of those exciting days Nat had a chance to share with us that morning. I hoped that our paths would cross again, but unfortunately they never did. I've always been sorry that I didn't get a chance to visit with Nat down in Tucson, Arizona, before he passed on in 1988.

That afternoon, I climbed aboard a DC-3 in McGrath, flew to Anchorage and then south to Seattle, glad that the summer's work was over, but more excited than ever about bush flying. I was feeling pretty proud of myself, but my initiation as a bush pilot was not yet complete. I still had a lot to learn, as I discovered four years later, this time not in Alaska, but in a remote area on the edge of Canada's great northwest wilderness, working for one of the most remarkable men I have ever met.

Chapter 14

Summer of '56

I felt more alive during the two summers I flew for the Coast and Geodetic Survey in Alaska than I had at any other time in my life. I don't know if it was because of the sense of freedom I felt or the way the challenge of the rugged terrain and the unpredictable weather got my adrenaline going. Whatever the reason, after that experience, it was really hard for me to settle back down into my old routine. Somehow I managed to finish college and went to work for Kenmore Air Harbor as chief mechanic and support pilot. This was the job I had dreamed about and hoped for since I was fifteen years old. But even this didn't quell the strange new restlessness I was now feeling. So, in the summer of 1956, when Bob Munro asked me if I'd be interested in another bush-flying assignment, I responded with an enthusiastic "You bet!"

The truth is, my cousin had some reservations about giving me this assignment. It was not because he didn't have faith in my ability as a pilot. After all, at twenty-four, I now had six solid years of commercial flying experience under my belt. What concerned Bob was my limited bush-flying experience. He knew that I had learned a lot during my two summers flying in Alaska, but this new assignment required a different kind of bush flying, in an area with a terrain and weather system that even some seasoned bush pilots found challenging. However, Bob didn't have much choice. Neither he, nor Kenmore's chief pilot, Bill Fisk, could commit to the three months of cargo hauling that Kenmore's contract with a Canadian company called Northwest Ventures called for. So, in spite of their misgivings, after loading me up with plenty of instructions and advice, Bill and Bob sent me off to do the job.

Like the fjords of Norway or the southeast coast of Alaska, there is a stunning, stark beauty about the remote area that unfolded before me on that June evening in 1956, as I guided my Piper Super Cub through a towering, ice-age carved canyon toward Stewart, British Columbia. Stewart is Canada's northernmost ice-free port. It sits at the headwaters of the Portland Canal, surrounded by the majestic coastal range of mountains and the spectacular Cambria Ice Fields. To reach Stewart by air, you follow the Portland Canal from its mouth in the Pacific Ocean near Prince Rupert, inland some ninety miles (144 km) through a steep fjord.

The canyon walls on both sides of the canal rise abruptly at a sixty- to ninety-degree angle, soaring heavenward to heights of 5,000 feet (1,500 m) or more. From the valley floor to the timberline at about 3,500 feet (1,050 m), the walls are lined with huge trees, some reaching heights of 100 to 150 feet (30–45 m). The color of the water where the canal spills into the ocean at Prince Rupert is a rich, deep blue. By the time it reaches Stewart, tons of fine silt continually washed down by glacier rivers have turned it into a soft, milky blue.

As I guided my Super Cub through the canyon, I viewed the beauty with an appreciative, but wary eye. Stewart is only 750 miles (1,200 km) from Seattle, less than a day's flying time, but the rugged landscape I saw below me might as well have been on another planet. There were no familiar ribbons of roads, no friendly patchwork quilt of fields down there to offer me the promise of a safe place to set down in case of a forced landing. And if I had to set down, I wondered, would anyone ever be able to find me in this vast, uninhabited bush. Fortunately, I didn't have to find out. I reached Stewart, without incident, at about seven-thirty that evening, under an almost cloudless azure sky. There was still another three or four hours of twilight left. Deep purple shadows moved across the face of the mountains. The setting sun, deflecting off the permanent ice fields that crowned the northern slopes, backlit the dark peaks with a shimmering, translucent aura of crimson and gold.

As instructed, I located a small hangar built on floats along the steep shoreline southwest of town, and brought my pontoon-fitted Super Cub 5314 Kilo in for a water landing. The weather was perfect. Just a two- or three- (3.2- or 4.8-km) mile-an-hour wind ruffling the surface. I taxied over to the hangar. Unfolding myself from the cabin of the two-seater, I stepped out onto the float. A Royal Canadian Mounted Policeman was waiting. The officer presented an imposing figure in his immaculate blue and red pants and tunic, and a peaked cap that added a good six inches (15 cm) to his already intimidating height. His unexpected presence unnerved me.

"Good evening, sir." The Mountie's tone was crisp. "What exactly are you doing here in Stewart?" He peered into the Cub's cabin. Canadians didn't take kindly to unauthorized American pilots operating in their territory.

Fortunately, I had the correct answer to his question. I produced a telegram from the Canadian Department of Transport. It gave my employer, Kenmore Air Harbor, permission to operate from a base in Stewart that summer. The permission had been granted because Northwest Ventures, a new Canadian corporation, needed someone to fly supplies off the water into a mining exploration site on a nearby glacier, but couldn't find a Canadian company willing to take on the job. Not that I could blame the Canadian companies. Landing with pontoons on a glacier is a risky maneuver. Few pilots had ever tried it, including me. However my cousin Bob and Bill Fisk had made successful runs of this nature on the other side of the same glacier for the Granby Mining Company, the developers of the Granduc Mine, in 1953 and 1954, using two Noordynn Norsemen. That job called for hauling supplies off barges in the Hyder area. Since Bob and Bill had to fly off the salt water, skis or wheels were not an option.

"Of course, they said it couldn't be done," Bob used to tell people, always with a laugh. "Foolish to even try it with floats. No way to get enough angle attack to lift off. Well, sir, I knew going downhill the wing would pick up enough speed to fly." He made it sound simple, but weighing the considerable instructions I had been given about glacier flying, I knew it wasn't going to be quite that easy.

Anyway, the Mountie inspected my papers. Satisfied that I was there on legitimate business, he departed. A few minutes later Tommy McQuillan, the fifty-five-year-old prospector who owned Northwest Ventures, came strolling down the gangway. The bespectacled, sandy-haired prospector was a husky, compact man, about five feet and seven inches (168 cm) and weighing in at around 160 pounds (72 kg). With his rolling gait and that roguish Irish grin of his, he reminded me of a slightly oversized leprechaun.

Tommy helped me guide the Super Cub into the hangar, which had been specially fitted with cutouts for pontoons. It belonged to the Granby Mining Company, but we had permission to use it when their planes weren't there. After securing the aircraft, Tommy and I loaded my gear into his jeep and headed for town.

It was a dusty ride. Any time Stewart experiences more than two consecutive days without rain, dust covers everything. But, as I learned that summer, this doesn't happen often. Prince Rupert may be Canada's rainiest city, but Stewart runs a close second. And the area is the uncontested champion for snowfall, thanks to Tide Lake, just thirty-one miles (50 km) north of town. Until recently, Tide Lake held the Guinness World Record for snowfall in one year. Between May 16, 1971, and May 15, 1972, eighty-nine feet (27 m) of snow reportedly fell in the region. (This record was eventually toppled by Mt. Rainier in my home state of Washington, which not too long ago managed to log a whopping ninety-nine feet (30 m) of snow in one year.)

But this was summer. Dust, not snow, coated Stewart's streets and the false fronts of its crumbling, weather-worn wood buildings. The town resembled the set of an old Wild West movie, especially around its favorite "watering hole." Like most of the other wooden structures in Stewart, the dilapidated tavern had been built quickly during a brief boom period in the early 1900s. Nothing much had been done to it since. Judging from the raucous sounds coming from inside as Tommy and I drove by, this fact had no effect on business. The miners and lumbermen, fresh down from the high country, were celebrating their hard-earned R and R with an abandon that would have made the patrons of any Wild West saloon feel right at home.

As we passed through town, I noticed an occasional pocket of new construction: a house here, a commercial building there; harbingers of a brand-new boom that was just about to take off. I learned later that the affable Tommy McQuillan had played a significant role in launching this new boom. In 1948, Tommy and a man named Einar Kvale located and staked out the high-grade copper deposit on the Leduc Glacier. Four years later, they optioned the property to Granby Mining, who developed it into what became known as the Granduc Mine. Over the next twenty-five years, that mining operation created thousands of well-paying jobs that drew adventurous Canadians to Stewart from all over the country. It also helped make Tommy a rarity in the prospecting business—a millionaire.

Tommy drove on to a small U-shaped lumber worker's cabin. According to Kenmore Air Harbor's contract with him, I would be going back and forth between Seattle and Stewart in roughly two-week cycles. During my two weeks home I would continue putting in my usual fourteen-hour days as a flight instructor, charter pilot and general airplane maintenance man. During my two weeks in Canada, I would stay with Tommy in this little cabin.

The cabin had a main room and kitchen, bracketed on each end by a very small, cot-fitted bedroom. As soon as we got inside, Tommy pointed to the bedroom that would be mine and told me to stow my gear while he cooked up something for us for dinner. He turned out to be a pretty good cook. Nothing fancy, just good, solid stick-to-your-ribs food, which was okay with me.

After dinner, Tommy laid out the plan for the next day's work. I was definitely going to earn my money on this job. The prudent thing would have been to retire early, but I wasn't feeling particularly prudent. I was too excited. The next day's challenges kept playing over and over again in my head. But that wasn't the only reason I lingered over my coffee. One of the things I loved most about flying in the bush is the remarkable people you get to meet. There I was, sitting with a man who actually made his living, and a good one at that, pursuing the unconventional, free-wheeling lifestyle of a prospector. I wanted to find out everything I could about him. Tommy loved talking about the old-timers he had met over the years, but he was reluctant to talk about himself. However, beginning that evening, and over the next three months, I managed to piece together some fascinating facts about this quiet, gentle man.

One of the first things I learned about Tommy was that he was a gambler. I don't mean the kind who haunt the tables at Las Vegas. Tommy gambled on his hunches. He was like a bulldog. Once he got a hunch, he never let go. Take the Stikine Silver prospect, for example.

This story begins back in the spring of 1932. Tommy was thirty-one years old. After working all winter to put together money for provisions, he decided to take a prospecting trip up the Unik River.

Traveling solo, he picked up a boat with an outboard in the southeast Alaskan town of Ketchikan, loaded his provisions and followed the Behm Canal to the Unik River. The Unik is about as tough a piece of water as you'll ever find. That didn't bother Tommy. When he reached rapids, he poled his way through. When he reached falls—there were three of them—he packed the boat and provisions up to the next level on foot. Finally, after a few weeks, leaving his boat behind, Tommy hiked up into the high country and began prospecting.

By the end of the season, Tommy had located some rocks near McKay Lake that, he thought, might "kick a little." He packed them down to his boat and headed back down the Unik River and the Behm Canal to Ketchikan. From there he caught the steamer to Seattle and continued on to Vancouver, British Columbia. Sure enough, when he finally got his samples to the assay office in Vancouver, they did kick a little—more than a little. They showed a number of ounces per ton of silver, as well as a high value of gold.

All winter, Tommy worked hard to put together enough money for another trip up the Unik. The following spring, when the ice began to thaw in the high country, he went back to Ketchikan, got his boat, his motor and all of his provisions, and went back up the Behm and the Unik to stake his claim. But when Tommy reached McKay Lake in mid-June, he discovered that there were already stakes in the ground. The stakes belonged to the Premier Mining Company, a highly successful British-based operation with a large gold mine just outside of Stewart. Premier was unaware of Tommy's activities the previous spring. They had just seen this outcrop from the air and decided to land their Waco seaplane on the lake and stake the area. Premier had planted their stakes just one week before Tommy got there. That was 1933.

Another man might have been discouraged. Not Tommy. He took the experience in his stride and moved on to other things, but he always kept close tabs on what was happening with the property.

In the 1930s, the Premier Mining Company did so well with its other ventures that it never got around to developing the McKay Lake site. During World War II, the government's cap on the value of gold, plus a shortage of labor and supplies, made it unprofitable to mine. Premier temporarily closed down all of its operations. The company started up again briefly after the war, still ignoring the

McKay Lake property. Finally, in 1962, it went out of business. Thirty-two years after Tommy made his original trip up the Unik to stake out the area, he was finally able to set down his own stakes. With a partner, he established the Stikine Silver prospect. But the story doesn't end there.

Tommy was a prospector, not a miner. Over the next twenty-plus years, he and his partner optioned the Stikine Silver property to five different mining companies. Not one of them found the consistent high values of silver or gold that would have warranted mining the area. Still, Tommy never lost faith in the site. All his instincts told him that there was a rich vein there somewhere. The mining companies just weren't drilling in the right spot.

One day, in 1982, Tommy and I—by then we had partnered in a few projects—were walking down a street in Vancouver.

"Ted," he said, "you should buy some Stikine stock. It's just been put on the Vancouver Stock Exchange. It's at twenty-five cents a share."

"I think right now I'd rather put my money in our projects," I told him. Tommy shook his head. "Well, that's going to be something some day."

"Yeah," I said, "I'm sure you're right, Tommy." But I thought to myself, Tommy has had five major mining companies looking up there and not one of them found anything.

A short time after that conversation, Tommy turned the Stikine over to a sixth mining company. Within a year, one of its drills came back coated with gold, so much gold that it actually painted the outside of the drill rod. The stock shot up from twenty-five cents a share to seventy-five dollars a share. That was the beginning of what today is known as British Columbia's Golden Triangle. To give you an idea of how rich the area is, by the end of 1998, one of the mines in the region, the Eskay Creek Mine, owned by Homestake Canada Ltd., had produced 934,631 ounces (26,496,789 g) of gold and 45.5 million ounces (1.3 billion g) of silver from 502,794 tons (502,794,000 kg) of ore. Believe me, I never again mistrusted one of Tommy's hunches.

But, back to 1956. Actually, it was one of Tommy's hunches that brought Tommy and me together that year. Tommy was gambling that since he was able to find a high-grade copper deposit on one side of the Leduc Glacier, chances were that the vein would pop up again on the other side or underneath. He already had a drilling team on the far side of the glacier, drilling around the clock. What he needed was someone to fly supplies in to them. The supplies would have to be flown off the water, which meant finding someone willing to tackle the dicey maneuver of landing on a glacier with pontoons.

When I jumped at the chance to take on that job, I understood the risks involved. Bob and Bill had made them perfectly clear. It was just that they seemed to pale next to the irresistible lure of the challenge. Besides, I knew those risks were manageable. Bob and Bill had already proven that. And I was still young enough to believe that I could do anything that anyone else could do in an airplane.

The next morning, Tommy was up and had breakfast ready by six-thirty. By seven-thirty, we were down at the plane, loading up. I gassed the Cub lightly to allow for as much cargo as possible. It was only half an hour each way. I figured thirty to forty-five minutes of spare fuel would be plenty. I was in the air by eight o'clock.

I took off and climbed up over Hyder, Alaska, a little village about two miles (3.2 km) and one time zone over the border from Stewart. I had never been there, but I hoped to rectify that situation before the summer was over, so I could get a first-hand look at Hyder's well-known Glacier Inn, just outside of town.

The Inn is best known for its bar, or rather, something that takes place in its bar. The bar itself is a quaint, rustic room plastered from ceiling to floor with dollar bills and other small denominations of money from all over the world, signed and placed there by patrons who have passed through. A sort of "Kilroy was here," Alaskan style. As I understand it, the custom of plastering the walls with signed dollar bills got started during the gold rush days. Prospectors headed for the gold fields would sign a bill and place it on the wall or ceiling as a form of insurance. This way, if they failed to strike it rich and ended up broke, they could at least retrieve their signed legal tender on the way back and buy a drink. But it was what the prospectors did (and modern day adventurers still do) before going out into the bush that has made the Glacier Inn's little bar famous. I'm talking about the ritual of "getting Hyderized," a northwest rite of passage.

"Getting Hyderized" involves drinking a shot of "Clear Spring," a 190-proof Kentucky grain alcohol. To heighten the drama, the bartender usually spills a few drops of the brew on the bar and sets them afire. After downing the shot, the intrepid initiate is considered officially Hyderized and pronounced ready to brave a northwest winter, or anything else.

Continuing to climb, I passed over the valley. Everywhere I looked there were snow-dusted mountains rising out of ancient ice fields and massive glaciers flowing like great rivers of ice, slowly transforming themselves and the landscape around them. This spectacular frozen landscape is the result of several periods of glaciation. The most recent, the Fraser glaciation period, peaked around 14,000 years ago, a time when much of what we know today as British Columbia and Alaska was covered with ice.

My instructions were to follow the Salmon River to its source, the massive Salmon Glacier, the fifth largest glacier in Canada. From there I was to continue on to the Frank Mackie Glacier, another offshoot of the same extensive ice field. I found the Frank Mackie as described, climbed to about 6,500 feet (1,950 m), and went over a little pass. My destination loomed directly ahead of me, a challenging, valley-filling mound of snow and ice glistening like white diamonds in the morning sun: the Leduc Glacier.

Chapter 15

Glacier Flying

As I approached the glacier, I could see the tents of the drilling party below, as well as something else—something that had a sobering effect on my euphoria. Beneath me, spread over the ice in the shape of a cross, was the distinct outline of a DeHavilland Beaver aircraft, or, rather, what was left of one. I remembered a story Tommy had told me the night before. I had been so focused on what I was going to be doing the next day that the importance of it hadn't really registered at the time.

The previous spring, the Granby Mining Company had purchased a brand-new Beaver on wheel-skis. A fellow named Harold Kellough from Prince Rupert had agreed to be both the mechanic and pilot. A few weeks before I arrived in Stewart, Harold was flying a load of dynamite fuses over to the glacier. Visibility was down. As he came in for his landing, he missed his mark and hit just at the lip of the glacier. The dynamite fuses ignited. In a matter of seconds, all that was left of Harold and the Beaver was the tail, two wing tips and a big burn spot. The remains of that airplane wasn't the only reminder I had that summer of the risks involved in my job, but it was certainly the most persistent. The ghostly outline of that burned-out Beaver stared up at me every time I made my final approach to land on the glacier.

I looked for a potential landing area that would get me as close to the drilling camp as possible; I located one about a mile away from it. "Remember, you're going to be flying in the mountains. You're not going to have any horizon to judge the steepness of the slope." That warning came from Bob Munro—part of his final instructions before I left Seattle. "So the first thing you are going to have to do," he told me, "is fly near and level with where you want to land to get an altimeter reading. That will give you the height of the landing area."

Having someone tell you there wasn't going to be a horizon is one thing. Experiencing it from the cockpit of a plane flying at seventy miles (112 km) an hour into the side of a snow-and ice-covered mound of rock is quite another. I now had a visceral understanding of my cousin Bob's concern about my lack of glacier-flying experience.

Bob also cautioned that with summer approaching the snow would be melting. Therefore, it would probably be higher up on the glacier than when he had checked the job out a month earlier. I wondered if he had any idea how much higher. I certainly had not anticipated the steepness of my landing area.

As instructed, I brought the Piper Super Cub in near a spot I thought might work for a landing and took an altimeter reading. Bill Fisk had instructed me to take three passes before I tried to land: A high pass, to look for any obstructions or crevasses in the landing area, and a lower pass, simulating landing, but at a high enough altitude to make another go-around. This was so I could get a sense of how steep the slope was. Then I was to go around one more time and, if all looked right, land.

The base of the Leduc Glacier was probably somewhere around 3,000 to 3,500 feet (900–1,050 m); the landing area I selected was about 4,200 feet (1,260 m). I made my first high pass. Everything looked okay. I dropped to a lower altitude for a second pass, with takeoff flaps pulled on and carburetor heat on. At about an altitude of 4,200 feet (1,260 m), I started my simulated landing. But before I could pull up for my third pass, the snow started to come up. As the distance between the Cub and the mountain rapidly shrank, I added power. Then more power. But the snow kept on coming, faster and faster. I could feel my adrenaline surging; that familiar metallic taste in my mouth. Like it or not, there wasn't going to be any chance for a third go-around. I pushed the carburetor heat off and was at full throttle and takeoff flaps. Keeping my air speed at sixty-five miles (104 km) an hour, I was preparing to touch down when I remembered Tommy's caution.

"When landing on a glacier," the prospector had told me the

night before, "if you come to a stop with the plane heading uphill, the steps in the floats will keep the plane from skidding backward. The problem is, they will also make it very hard for you to turn the plane around by yourself." Tommy said the trick was to touch down and start a turn, but stop halfway through so the plane is pointed somewhat downhill for the takeoff.

As the plane started to slow down, I (with full throttle on) kicked the rudder pedal, turning the Cub to about a forty-five-degree angle, to position the plane partially facing downhill before it came to a stop. For a frightening moment, my old 5314 Kilo teetered dangerously, but it finally stabilized. I had made it! My first landing on a glacier, maybe not according to Hoyle, but at least in one piece. I quickly unloaded the supplies. There were two good-sized boxes of groceries, probably fifteen to twenty pounds (6–9 kg) of Blazo fuel and laundry—all the stuff of life that makes it possible to live in such a remote spot.

Looking down the glacier, I could see that it was a nice, steep descent. I waved back at the drillers who had watched me land from their drilling rig below and climbed back into the cockpit. Now all I had to do was take off.

The ease with which the engine turned over and started up surprised me. I had forgotten that the air is thinner at that altitude, resulting in less compression. The propeller pulled through rapidly. I checked the gauges, shut the side door, pushed the throttle ahead and started my descent down the steep, snowy slope. There were little rivulets in the snow; it was like riding railroad tracks in a car. The plane shook and racked sideways, to the left, then to the right, accelerating all the time. Before I knew it, I had the Cub up to flying speed. When you fly off a slope, you don't just pull back on the stick and ride the heel of the floats down the slope. You get up to your flying speed and gently lift off, almost parallel to the slope.

My second trip that day went without a hitch. When I returned to Stewart to pick up my third load, Tommy decided to come along to give me a hand. He probably figured that since I had made it back in one piece twice, it was safe to fly with me. It was still a beautiful day, with hardly any wind. The mountain peaks were just gorgeous. Having done some climbing when I was younger, I really appreciated being up in those mountains.

As we headed over the Frank Mackie Glacier, Tommy,

ensconced in the rear seat, pointed out where he had found the minerals that had helped trigger the Granduc mining venture. He also pointed out the route he and his crew had taken when they had hauled their mining equipment overland to the Leduc. It had been an arduous, circuitous, twenty-two-mile (35-km) trek over a 5,500-foot (1,650-m) pass and several glaciers, including the massive Salmon Glacier. I tried to visualize what their journey must have been like.

"Looks like it'd be tough enough to maneuver down there just toting normal climbing gear," I shouted over the drone of the engine. "How did you ever manage to haul equipment through there?"

"Just ran a chain of bulldozers with wanigans behind them," Tommy shouted back.

"Wanigans?"

"You know, those little storage buildings like they use up at the lumber camp. We put some runners on them and used them like sleds. Just took 'em right over the top and on down into the Leduc."

Tommy also told me about plans the government in British Columbia had to build an eleven-mile (18-km) tunnel from the road to the mine, so that the mine could be operated economically, and the workers could live in Stewart and go back and forth. The tunnel would have to be driven under mountain ridges and glaciers. It seemed like an impossible task to me, but Tommy was confident that it could be done, and eventually time proved him right.

I maneuvered the Cub through the pass and out over Harold's marker. By the time we landed on the Leduc, everything was feeling pretty routine. Tommy and I put a makeshift sled together, loaded it with supplies and equipment, and headed for the camp below.

In addition to the drilling equipment, the camp had three pyramid-shaped tents, each poised a few feet above the ground on a precarious pedestal of ice and snow. They looked as if a good wind would send them toppling. Tommy explained how the unusual configuration came about. He said that during the day, as the sun melted the ice and snow around the tents, the ice and snow beneath them, which got no sun, remained frozen. The more the ice around the tents melted, the higher the tents got. Each night the drillers chipped new steps into the pedestals so they could get up into their tents.

Nothing was easy for Tommy's drillers: the work was hazardous, the environment unfriendly and the accommodations primi-

159

tive. Because of the short summer season and the continuing movement of the glacier, the drill on the Leduc was operated day and night without interruption. To accomplish this, the drillers worked twelve-hour shifts—twelve hours on, twelve hours off. The challenge was compounded by the fact that neither Tommy nor his drillers had any experience drilling through a glacier. They were pioneering new territory.

It takes a hardy breed of man, tough mentally and physically, to function productively under such grueling conditions. Why did they do it, I wondered? Money, obviously, was part of the lure, as well as a sense of adventure. But, as I discovered in my conversations with the drillers, there was another reason. Many of them were there simply because the project was for Tommy.

That afternoon at the drilling camp, I witnessed for the first time Tommy's extraordinary rapport with his drilling crew. Technically he was the boss and they were his employees, but Tommy McQuillan didn't put much stock in technicalities. What you got when you signed on with him was not a boss-employee relationship, but true camaraderie. Tommy's management philosophy was to hire the best men available for the job, give them what they need to get it done, and treat them with the respect their skills deserved.

I sensed another, subtle, indefinable element to this formula. Maybe it was Tommy's ever-ready grin or the way he always gave you his full attention when you were talking with him. Whatever it was, Tommy had a way of making the people who worked for him feel that he really cared about them. In return, the men exhibited a loyalty to Tommy far beyond what any boss would have a right to expect. They not only accomplished the improbable for him, sometimes they even managed the impossible. And he never had to ask. I learned more about effective management that summer from this amiable Irishman than I learned in all the years that followed, from all the books I read and all the courses I took.

Once we delivered the mail and supplies, and Tommy had checked the drilling reports, we headed back to the Cub. The trek down had been a breeze. The 700-foot (210-m) vertical climb back up was another story.

I had always prided myself on my stamina, but by the time I reached the plane I was huffing and puffing like an overloaded steam engine. Looking back, I saw Tommy coming up behind me some 100 yards (91 m) down the slope. He wasn't even breathing heavy. He looked more like someone returning from a brisk stroll around the block than a fifty-five-year-old man who had just hiked more than a mile through ice and snow, straight up the side of a glacier.

I knew it wasn't just a matter of conditioning. After all, I was in good shape and a lot younger than Tommy. The difference, I learned after questioning the prospector, was in philosophy. In my youthful zeal, I had attacked the slope with a determination to conquer it. I had invested my full energy into every painstaking step. Tommy approached the climb the same way he approached life. He fixed his sights on his goal. Then, like the fabled racing tortoise, he proceeded at his own steady, unhurried pace, never stopping until he reached it. This was another lesson for me.

The Super Cub has just one two-piece door on the right-hand side. The top of the door, the glass portion, folds up to the wing, and the bottom folds down to the wing strip. Tommy climbed into the backseat, and I took my place in the front. We put on our seat belts, and I started up that reliable thirty-five horsepower engine, revving it up. I even did a little bit of a mag check. You couldn't give it a normal run up to 1,700 without sliding down the glacier, but I gave it a quick check. Then I closed the door, opened the throttle, and off we went.

I made a few more freight runs to the Leduc Glacier that afternoon. The weather remained beautiful all day, but by evening a few high clouds had come in. With his savvy of the country, Tommy told me that he figured we would be able to get some flying in during the morning, but the weather would probably turn shabby by afternoon. This was okay with him as he had some special plans for the next afternoon anyway. He was going to Stewart for the wedding of one of the local belles. It was an important event, and nearly everyone in town was going. Since there isn't a lot in the way of entertainment out in the bush, a celebration like this is always given top priority.

In addition to dropping off supplies at the drill camp, Tommy wanted to check out a few locations where he planned to do some prospecting later in the week, so when I gassed up the next morning I topped off the tanks. We climbed on up the glacier valley, climbed on to the Frank Mackie Glacier. As we headed over the pass, the clouds were already beginning to come down, but they were dropping slowly.

The pass was still open when we left the camp on the Leduc and headed for our first prospecting survey site. However, Tommy, an old hand at mountain flying, knew how fickle the weather could be. And he had no intention of missing that wedding.

"Listen," he shouted, "I don't like the looks of this weather. Let's go ahead and scrub the rest of the trip. We'll just hit McKay Lake and head straight back to Stewart."

The lake was some thirty to forty miles (48–64 km) to the north, about fifteen to twenty minutes of flying time. I headed the Cub down the Unik Valley and then cut in close to the peaks on the right, in a northeasterly direction. As I did, I noticed that the clouds were beginning to settle more rapidly. Tommy looked back up the Unik River. The news was bad. Everything had closed in behind us. There was no chance of getting back to Stewart the way we had come. Our only choice was to continue ahead.

We checked out McKay Lake as planned and I turned and headed the Cub up the middle fork of the Unik River to where it almost joins the Bear River. My plan was to follow the Bear, which winds its way around to pass behind Stewart, but I was too late. The rapidly descending clouds had closed that pass, too. Stewart was to the northeast, but I knew that the only chance I had to get Tommy back in time for that wedding now was to fly northwest, then southwest, out toward Ketchikan, down the Behm Canal in the United States and back up the Portland Canal. So I headed northwest.

Up until this point the weather had been relatively calm. The wind wasn't blowing; there was no turbulence. But as we approached Boundary Lake, it began to rain.

Tommy decided that since we were so close, he would check on a little cabin he had built on the lake's edge, his favorite spot in the whole region. I touched down and taxied up into the rushes in front of the cabin. It was a sturdy structure. I marveled at the craftsmanship reflected in the construction, especially knowing that Tommy had built it all by himself from scratch, with only the few tools he was able to carry in by boat. He hadn't visited the place for some time. A quick look inside revealed that aside from the usual signs of mice and pack rats, it was in good shape and well stocked with food.

We both went outside the cabin and looked up at the sky. It was evident that the weather wasn't going to clear up behind us for some time, and we had no way of knowing what lay ahead. Under other circumstances, we would probably have stayed there and waited out the weather, but Tommy had a wedding to go to. So we decided to head for the Behm Canal to work our way back to Stewart.

We taxied out into Boundary Lake, the center of which, Tommy claimed, marked the boundary between Alaska and Canada. Something, he said with a twinkle in his eye, that he found very useful. If the rules of one country were more restrictive about something than the rules of the other, he could always just go by boat or foot to the country with the least restrictive rules. Years later, of course, it was decided that Boundary Lake wasn't a boundary at all, but Canadian territory. However it made a great story at the time.

By the time we reached the Behm Canal, the rain was coming down hard. Visibility had dropped to about three to three-and-a-half miles (5–5.6 km). The wind had picked up to thirty or forty knots. The Cub was a ninety- to 100-mile-an-hour (144- to 160-km) plane. With that kind of headwind, we were only able to make about fifty to sixty knots.

I had been hugging the water to avoid the clouds so I could keep visibility in case I had to turn around or land, but now the waves were running five- to six-feet (1.5- to 1.8-m) high. If the engine quit, there was no way I would be able to land on the water. I would have to take my chances on the rocky shoreline or, if I was lucky, find a little bay. It was now a little after noon. We had started out from Stewart before seven in the morning.

The weather over the Behm Canal finally cleared a little, but that advantage vanished when we reached Dixon Entrance. As I began my turn to enter the Portland Canal, which runs parallel to the Behm at this point, some five miles (8 km) away, I hit a relentless wall of turbulence. Fifty-five- to sixty-mile-an-hour (88- to 96-km) winds hammered at the Cub, tossing it around as if it were a toy. It was like being on a runaway roller coaster. My stomach responded accordingly. However, I figured that with all that headwind, once I managed to make it around the bend I'd probably have a good tailwind for the ninety-mile (144-km) straight run up the Portland Canal to Stewart. But I was wrong.

There was a brief, small tailwind, and visibility did improve to about seven miles (11 km) right after the turn. But within ten minutes flying time everything changed. The tailwind disappeared, the ceiling started dropping. Before I knew it, visibility was down to a mile. I lowered my altitude to about fifty feet (15 m) off the water and slowed down my speed, just in case we encountered any fishing boats coming down the canal. Tommy checked his watch. It was two o'clock. The wedding was at five. To compound our problems, the Cub's fuel tanks were now down to less than half full, and we still had about seventy miles (112 km) to go.

The ceiling continued to drop. I put on partial flaps, touched on the water and taxied on the step. The Cub was now traveling at about thirty miles (48 km) an hour. With visibility rapidly deteriorating, I began to hug the shoreline to keep some sense of where I was. Since I had no way of knowing where a promontory might be sticking out, I slowed down off the step to normal taxi speed.

We crawled along like this for a nerve-racking hour, both of us straining to see what was up ahead. Finally, Tommy climbed out of his backseat, slid underneath the airplane to the spreader bars that separated the floats, then onto the left float. Holding onto the left-wing strut, he peered at the edge of the canal, calling out warnings whenever he spotted potential danger.

We taxied along at this snail's pace for another hour. Visibility was now down to 100 feet (30 m). It was three o'clock. Without a little luck, chances of making the wedding were beginning to look slim.

Finally, about twenty miles (32 km) from Stewart, visibility began to pick up. Tommy slipped under the airplane and slid into his seat. I went back to taxiing on the step. At four o'clock, we were about ten miles (16 km) from Stewart, doing twenty to twenty-five miles (32–40 km) an hour. At the five-mile (8-km) point, the visibility was good enough for me to get the Cub back in the air. When we finally landed at the hangar in Stewart, I tied down the plane while Tommy dashed off to the wedding. He made it with twenty minutes to spare.

The distance from Stewart to the Leduc Glacier is normally about thirty minutes flying time; as a straight line, probably only twenty-five or thirty miles (40–48 km). McKay Lake is another thirty to forty miles (48–64 km) to the north. But to get there and back on that day, Tommy and I had logged more than 220 exhausting air and sea miles (352 km).

Chapter 16

Initiation Completed

Over the next three days, a series of storms pounded the region. I went down to the hangar every morning to ensure the Cub was safe and snug in its mooring. But once that was done, there was nothing else for me to do. Restlessly, I wandered around town in the rain in search of an antidote for my boredom. Jack Crowhurst, manager of the Granby Mining Company, finally came to my rescue. His employers owned two aircraft on wheels: a Grumman Widgeon, which one of their pilots ferried back and forth between Stewart and Vancouver, B.C., and a Fairchild 82.

The Fairchild wasn't the familiar twin-boom military airplane used to carry troops. It was the big brother of the Fairchild 71, a single-engine, high-wing, eight-place aircraft resembling a Norseman, with room for two people in front and a good-sized cargo compartment. To accommodate the two planes, an airstrip had been fashioned from the delta of the Bear River. Gravel had been smoothed out and punched down to create a 2,500-foot (750-m) runway, and construction had just been completed on a hangar. Jack needed someone to backfill the area around the newly built hangar. The job required braving the unfriendly elements on the company's D-4 Cat.

The weather didn't concern me. Neither did the fact that I had never operated a Cat. If anything, that heightened my interest. I have always found any unmastered piece of equipment an irresistible challenge. So, with Tommy's blessings, I volunteered and spent the next day out in the rain, happily pushing around wet gravel.

That evening, to help ease my boredom, Tommy decided it was

time to introduce me to Stewart's nightlife. Since my arrival, the prospector had purposely avoided the dilapidated wooden tavern about three blocks on the water-side of the town's main hotel. Even though he knew I wasn't a drinking man, he worried that any late-night partying might compromise the sharp edge he felt I needed to manage the potential risks I faced every time I took off from Stewart. However, now that I was grounded by the weather, he saw no harm in my soaking up a little local color.

The smoke-filled tavern was packed to the rafters with its usual boisterous assemblage of miners, lumbermen and prospectors. I followed Tommy to the bar. Everyone was drinking Molson Blue. The bartender raised an eyebrow when I ordered a 7UP. Even though Tommy had predicted more rain, eternal optimist that I was, I figured that there was still an outside chance that tomorrow might turn out to be a flying day. I decided not to risk a hangover, just in case.

We had no sooner settled ourselves into a couple of well-worn captain's chairs in a corner of the room when a lanky Scandinavian, his slicker still moist from the rain, sidled up to our table. From the weathered face atop the six-feet-and-three-inch (188-cm) frame, I guessed him to be somewhere in his mid-sixties. His hands were massive, with long thick, scarred fingers. He stopped directly in front of me.

"Vood yew mind standing up?"

I looked at Tommy. The Irishman just smiled and nodded. By the time I reached my feet, the decibel level in the room had fallen to a whisper. I didn't have to look around to know that all eyes were on me.

The stranger squinted at me for a moment. Then, reaching under his slicker, into the pocket of his bib-style Levi's, he produced a tape measure and proceeded to measure me from head to toe. The room resonated with laughter.

"Tank yew," the man said. He returned his tape measure to his pocket and departed. The crowd resumed its drinking. Face still flushed, I slipped back into my chair, with a questioning look at Tommy.

"That was Lars," Tommy said. "He's a cabinetmaker."

I didn't understand.

"He also makes caskets for the local undertaking establishment.

I guess with all the problems we've been having with pilots crashing around here this year, he just wants to be prepared."

That was my second reminder to stay alert on my little forays out to the glacier.

The weather finally broke. Fresh snow graced the peaks. Raindrops, trapped in the limbs of the towering evergreens, sparkled in the sun like Christmas lights. The rain-washed sky was a brilliant blue. Once again I took to the air.

Each time that summer that I began my climb out toward the glacier, just around the corner above Stewart I would pass over what looked like the remains of a ski lift. When I asked Tommy about it he told me it was actually an old work cart, part of an eleven-mile (18-km) aerial tramline that used to carry gold bearing ore from the gold mine in the hillside down to tidewater. According to Tommy, in its day it had been one of the longest tramlines on the continent. But what I found fascinating about that old tramline was the route it had to take. The mine and the dock from which the ore was shipped out were both in Canada. However, because of the location of the mine, right there on the U.S.-Canadian border, to get the ore from the mine to the wharf, the tram had to first go through Alaska. I wondered if every load they sent down had to go through customs as it passed from one country to the other, but Tommy said back in the 1930s when the old tramline was in operation, the customs people didn't bother too much about checking every bucket.

The tramline belonged to the Premier Mine, started back in 1910 by a British mining company. It was a pretty successful operation for many years. In 1921, the property shipped 6,000 tons (6 million kg) of ore with the gold valued at 1.5 million Canadian dollars. But by the time I got to Stewart in 1956, Premier only had a small operation going—some twelve to fourteen miners, whereas they once employed 300 to 400.

I flew on past the Premier, over the Frank Mackie and on to the Leduc. Harold's reminder at the bottom of the glacier was still in place as I went in for another landing. I touched down in the snow, turned around and slid to a stop, unloaded the freight and quickly took off again for Stewart.

On the way back to Stewart that afternoon, I noticed that things were pretty busy on the other side of the Leduc. The Granby Mining Company had begun work on their above-ground facilities to start mining underground. There was also some activity that I suspect had to do with the proposed tunnel the government was planning to build under the glacier between Stewart and the mine. It seemed strange to see this beehive of activity unfold in this pristine area that only a short time ago had been devoid of any human activity.

Later in the afternoon, after I had delivered my fifth load to the Leduc and grabbed a quick sandwich, I flew Tommy over to McKay Lake to the Stikine silver outcrop. Tommy picked up a few samples and checked out an area in the high country where he was going to bring in a couple of other prospectors to do some additional evaluation. After being grounded by the weather for three days, it was good to be flying again.

There was plenty to keep me challenged that summer. In addition to flying supplies to the drilling camp, Tommy had me bring in a set of wheels on one of my trips home so we could check out a couple of locations in the interior where he planned to do some prospecting.

It was interesting how we got those wheels on the Cub. At high tide we put a sled out in the mouth of the river where there were a couple of posts sticking up. I taxied the airplane up and tied it to the two posts so that it would be over the sled. Then when the tide went out, the sled was sitting there with the Super Cub on top of it. We connected the sled to that DF caterpillar tractor and pulled it up to the hanger. We got out a hoist, undid the nuts and bolts, held the airplane out of the floats, lifted it up in the air and put the landing gear on it. Then I filled the brake lines, checked the brakes, put on the tail wheel and taxied out, and we were flying a land plane.

On those trips into the interior, we would land on small-village air strips, fuel up and take off again, sometimes flying eight or nine hours in a day. I also carried out a mission of mercy that summer. A young man working for the mining company nearly severed two of his fingers in an accident in the hills. I flew him to Smithers for medical treatment.

As the summer wore on, my glacier flying became increasingly difficult. When the melting snow made the tents at the drilling camp unstable, they simply moved them. But there was nothing I could do about the shrinking snow cap that made my landing site steeper and steeper with each passing day. Fortunately, the transition was a gradual one, so the risk remained manageable. However, toward the end of the summer, I was reminded once again of how real that risk was.

The year of 1956 was a special international geophysical year. A joint expedition of scientists from Russia, America and New Zealand was working on the Frank Mackie Glacier. While I was in Seattle for one of my two weeks off, a pilot named Will and a Swiss national who worked for the Granby Mining Company took off in the company's Fairchild 82 to make some airdrops of equipment to the expedition. On this particular day, visibility was good and there was no wind to speak of. However, the weather had been exceptionally warm.

The problem with warm weather is that it can affect an aircraft's performance. Under standard temperature conditions, air can support a plane at slower speeds, but as the temperature rises, the molecules in the air move farther apart so that there are fewer molecules per square cubic foot of air. This reduced density translates into less lift for the wings. The thinner air also affects engine performance, reducing pressure in the cylinder. This means less available horsepower. In this instance the problem was compounded because Will was flying at a high altitude, where the air is already thinner, and was dealing with a steep hill and a heavy load.

Will brought his plane in low for the drop. As the Swiss national began releasing the equipment, the pilot noticed that the Fairchild was losing altitude. The hill was outclimbing him.

"We're going to go in," he warned his companion.

Evidently the idea of a crash landing didn't appeal to the Swiss gentleman. Instead of moving back to the cabin and strapping himself in for the impact, he followed the freight right out through the hole. The Fairchild staggered, went over on its wing and dumped in on the snow. Jumping prematurely didn't help the Swiss. He and Will were equally broken up in the mishap. Fortunately, they both recovered in a reasonable period of time. The same can't be said for the Fairchild. It was scattered all over the Frank Mackie.

A few weeks later, I had good cause to recall Will's misfortune. It was a gray day with slowly descending clouds. The weather made me uneasy as I flew through the pass on my way to the Leduc. I made my freight drop at the drilling camp, landing and taking off as quickly as I could. Unfortunately, the weather was moving more quickly. As I headed back toward Stewart, I could still see the top of the pass, but by the time I reached it, the weather had moved in up against the mountain. Luckily, I could still see down the Frank Mackie Glacier.

I made a rapid descent down the face of the hill. It was a gamble, but I thought that if I got lower, I would be able to slip under the flat base of the clouds I had just flown under fifteen minutes earlier. At that time the clouds had a base of about 6,000 feet (1,800 m), just touching the top of the pass. I didn't think that they could be any lower than another 1,000 feet (300 m) by the time I got back. But I thought wrong.

As I got further down in the pass, I discovered that I couldn't return to get back up. Using the dark rocks on the sides of the hill as reference points, I continued down the mountain, hoping for improved visibility. I didn't find it. Finally, I worked my way down on top of the Frank Mackie Glacier. Unlike the Leduc, the Frank Mackie is a relatively flat glacier. I knew if I was forced to land on it, there was no way I would be able to get off again. The Super Cub didn't have enough horsepower to accelerate for liftoff in the snow without more downslope.

As I rolled down over to the top of the Frank Mackie, I could see the tents of the geophysical party a half-mile ahead. Using them as a reference point, I flew just above the snow with my flaps set for landing. A queasy feeling began developing in my stomach; I was quickly running out of options. I didn't want my Cub to become another marker like Harold's Beaver or Will's Fairchild. I certainly didn't want Lars to have to use the measurements he took that stormy evening in the pub. These thoughts prompted a decision. If I couldn't keep my perception of the horizon well enough, I would touch down in the snow. I might be stuck, but at least I would be stuck close to other human beings. I'd worry about solving the problem of getting my airplane out of there later.

Flying by the tents, I noticed a set of tracks going up the glacier. I turned and followed the footprints. My adrenaline was really flowing now! It looked like there was no way I was going to be able to avoid touching down. That's when I saw the figures standing in the snow, like a grouping of pylons set in a cloud. They were just the reference point I needed. I swung off to the right, so I could keep them in view. The startled scientists looked up in amazement as my small green Super Cub made a turn around them and disappeared down the glacier into the clouds.

My confidence was building. If I could get oriented and get down the glacier far enough, I was now certain I could get out from underneath the low clouds. After all, I had only been in the air maybe twenty minutes from the time I had excellent visibility over the Frank Mackie Glacier. I followed the footprints back down the glacier, past the camp. It seemed like an eternity, but it was probably only four or five minutes before I came out of the mist and found the base for the clouds. This gave me fifteen to twenty miles (24–32 km) of visibility as I worked my way back to Stewart.

The next couple of days went by without a break in the weather. With time on my hands, I continued to pump Tommy about his life and his work. I learned that the Irishman had grown up on Vancouver Island, in Courtenay, British Columbia. His father owned and operated a livery stable. Tommy, who was the oldest child, worked in the family business along with his brothers and sisters. But he was a restless young man. When news of another gold rush in Alaska reached town, he signed up as a seaman on a steamship headed for Alaska. After a few cruises on the inside passage, they reached Juneau, and Tommy left the ship to become a miner.

In Juneau, Tommy learned how to sort gold ore from the large amount of tailings that were coming out of the Juneau mine. Juneau is also where his love affair with rocks began. He became fascinated by what rocks can tell you when you look at them closely. Most at home in the outdoors, he headed for the wilderness, trapping all winter to earn enough money so he could prospect in the summer.

In the early years, while he was still learning his trade, Tommy worked with other prospectors, going back into the remote areas, living off the land. He had a great respect for those hardy men and loved to tell stories about them, or retell tales he had learned from them over the years. Eventually, Tommy began to work alone more and more. Whenever he would go into a new area, he would build himself a cabin. He had a string of them in remote areas throughout the region.

Tommy was always happiest when he was prospecting. However, as he explained to me on one of our survey trips that summer, his chosen profession was not without its risks. The area we were checking out at the time was thick with underbrush and loaded with devil's club, an unfriendly plant with leaves about two to three feet (.6–.9 m) in diameter and a thick stalk studded with an inch-and-a-half to two-inch (3.75- to 5-cm) thorns. The ground was wet. It almost always is in that area of British Columbia. I thought I heard a noise. I asked Tommy if there were bears in the area. The Irishman grinned and recalled an experience he had several years earlier not too far away, on the south fork of the Unik River. It was during a prospecting trip he had taken with a young partner named Charlie.

"We had just set up our tent on this game trail," he told me. "I put a roll of paper under my arm and headed out into the woods. I had just taken my trousers down and was squatting when I heard this deep noise: 'Uhhhnnn!' Well, sir, I knew it wasn't me ... so I hastily gathered up my pants and hightailed it out of there right through the bush, thorns and all, yelling to Charlie, 'Get the gun! Get the gun, Charlie!' because I could hear that bear coming up fast, right behind me.

"Clutching my suspenders under my chin, I flew over the fallen logs at the edge of camp, right past Charlie. Charlie was down on one knee, rifle to shoulder, eyes fixed on the underbrush. Before I could grab my gun out of the tent, that bear—a huge grizzly—came flying over the logs. Charlie let go with a shot and hit him right between the eyes. The grizzly died on the spot. Still clutching my suspenders, I swung around just in time to see the grizzly drape itself over the logs. Charlie turned to me. I could see he was badly shaken.

"'Tom,' he said, 'don't you ever, ever bring a bear into camp again!'"

That Tommy McQuillan was a great storyteller.

Prospecting is a hit-or-miss occupation, usually more miss than hit, but Tommy had a special talent for it. He had an uncanny ability for sniffing out pay dirt in places where others saw nothing. I witnessed that talent firsthand that summer. The Premier Mining Company had concluded that there wasn't enough gold left in one of its mines to make continued operation worthwhile. The company decided to lease the mine out. Tommy found out about it and went to have a look. He took me with him.

I followed Tommy around as he examined the property and inspected the adits. To my untutored eye, Premier appeared to be right. The mine certainly looked played out. Others had also checked the mine and found nothing promising. But something apparently caught Tommy's eye, because he went out, found himself three partners and leased the property.

The following year I learned that Tommy and his partners had brought out more than one million dollars worth of gold from that mine. The four men did all the work themselves by hand. They hauled the ore out by jeep, put it in a dump truck and drove it down to Stewart. That cinched it for me. I knew then and there that I wanted to, and shortly afterward did, partner with the "lucky" prospector.

But back to 1956. There was one incident that summer that briefly shook my faith in my newfound mentor. We had finished our work in Stewart and Tommy asked me to fly him back to Vancouver in the Cub. He certainly could have afforded to go by airline. There was one that flew out of Stewart, and the flight would have been more comfortable. But like me, Tommy had a great love for small planes. In fact, he had flown himself in his younger days. The only reason he was no longer a pilot was that he had decided his real interest was in prospecting. Wisely, he realized he couldn't do both things well.

It was already late morning by the time we finished loading our bags and the landing gear we had used for the wheel-work into the Cub, and took off for Vancouver on floats. We stopped to gas up in Prince Rupert and Bella Bella, and by the time we reached Comox the sun was already beginning to set.

"There's no way we will make Vancouver before dark," I told Tommy. "We'd better land here." Tommy was delighted. "Then we can drop in on a girlfriend of mine," he announced.

Now, you have to understand that over the summer, Tommy had become my hero ... a man I wanted to emulate. Among the things I had come to admire about the Irishman was his absolute devotion to his wife. He told me that he met Betty on a Union Steamship. She was on her way back to Vancouver after spending the Christmas holidays in Stewart with some friends who worked for the Premier Mine. It was love at first sight, Tommy said, and he insisted that after three decades of marriage, Betty was still the light of his life. So you can see why the discovery that he had a girlfriend upset me.

As soon as we landed in the bay at Courtenay, Tommy hailed a taxi, hustled me into it, and we were on our way. During the short ride, my sense of unease continued to build. The dalliances of a married man, especially one so "mature," was something I had no desire to witness, but it looked like I wasn't going to have any choice.

The cab pulled up in front of an old two-story wooden house in good repair, with a well-cared for garden. When we reached the porch, Tommy knocked crisply on the front door, then turned and winked at me. He seemed to be enjoying my discomfort. After a moment the porch light came on. A second later the door opened, and a woman emerged out of the shadows and threw her arms around Tommy.

"Ted," the Irishman said with a grin, as he disengaged himself, "I'd like you to meet my mother."

"Pleased to meet you, ma'am," I stammered. I could feel my face flush with embarrassment as I reached out to shake the extended hand of the sweet-faced, little white-haired lady smiling at me. Out of the corner of my eye I could see Tommy still grinning. "Gotcha!" that grin said.

Learning to land and take off from a glacier, and navigating a float plane through zero visibility that summer rounded out my initiation as a bonafide bush pilot. It was also some of the most exciting flying I have ever done. But I think my most vivid memories of those three months are of the times I shared with Tommy and all the things the experienced prospector taught me, not just about prospecting, but also about nature and life. We remained friends and partnered in numerous ventures in the years that followed until Tommy's death in 1989 at the age of ninety-one. The Irishman continued to prospect up until two years before his passing.

The phrase is often an exaggeration, but in Tommy McQuillan's case, the man did indeed became a legend in his own time. No one knew or loved the Canadian northwest wilderness better than Tommy. He must have walked nearly every accessible inch of the territory, and some not so accessible. With a tenacious spirit, a contagious lust for life and a quiet, unassuming courage, he left behind a legion of admirers. Some, like me, knew him as a mentor. They shared Tommy's love of the wilderness and were attracted by his integrity and good nature. There were others who owed Tommy their lives. Occasionally, as he tracked over the harsh, rugged terrain, he would come across some less experienced adventurer caught off-guard by the elements or insufficiently prepared for the dangers; men who would have perished in the wilderness had Tommy not come by and rescued them, sometimes with a calculable risk to his own safety.

As a tribute to this man who left such an indelible mark on the land he so loved, a group of surveyors mapping the region named a mountain ridge after him. Appropriately, McQuillan Ridge straddles a piece of land at the junction of the south fork and the main channel of the Unik River.

After Tommy's death, one of his admirers arranged to have Tommy's wife, his brother, Ray, and me flown to McQuillan Ridge in a chartered helicopter so we could scatter Tommy's ashes there. We waited in Stewart two days for the weather to clear. When it finally did, the day was magnificent! It was as though the wilderness had turned out in all its splendor to welcome home this gentle, kindred spirit.

We headed out past the Granduc Mine, now closed, toward the ridge, and Betty got her first look at the only other passion in her husband's life: the great northwest wilderness region she had unselfishly shared him with during their nearly half-century marriage. I had a special brass plaque bearing Tommy's likeness made for the occasion. When we touched down on McQuillan Ridge, we released Tommy's ashes and Ray and I fastened the plaque to a large rock. It is still there today, designating the spot as "McQuillan Ridge." The plaque reads: "Tommy McQuillan, 1898–1989. Persevering, kind, he opened up the country."

My two summers flying for the Coast and Geodetic Survey in Alaska and my summer working for Tommy in British Columbia not only allowed me to earn my stripes as a bush pilot, but also marked the beginning of what has been for me a rich, exciting and rewarding career in aviation. In my twenties and early thirties, I landed on glaciers with floats and skis from British Columbia to Mt. McKinley. I towed banners in Germany, flew lookout for forest fires in Idaho, and towed gliders with eighty-five horsepower Cubs in the Paloose hills of Washington.

Eventually, I realized my boyhood dream of becoming an airline pilot, a profession I enjoyed for thirty-two years. My first job was for Pacific Northern Airlines (PNA). PNA's founder, Art Woodley, was a tough bush pilot with a heart of gold. He really cared about the people of PNA and its customers. We out-carried all of our competitors to any destination in Alaska. The small, pioneering PNA, with just 600 employees, was eventually gobbled up by Western Airlines, which in turn was gobbled up by Delta Air Lines. Bush flying will always be my first love, but my airline days have given me some wonderful memories, too. I've landed a Boeing 727 above the Arctic Circle in Deadhorse, Alaska, at fifty degrees below zero (–45°C), and in Mexico City at ninety degrees Fahrenheit (32°C). I remember one night, flying the familiar route from Seattle to Anchorage, looking out of the cockpit window and seeing the Alaskan sky ablaze with the brilliant colors of the aurora borealis. I thought to myself, I can't believe they actually pay us to do this.

I've thought about it a lot, but I can't imagine what my life would have been like if I couldn't fly. Perhaps you have to be a pilot to understand, but flying isn't just something someone does. It's really a way of life and it has a way of shaping how you look at the world.

I have been very fortunate. When I was twenty years old, a once-in-a-lifetime opportunity crossed my path, and somehow I managed to find the courage to risk looking foolish and go for it. As a result, all my life I have had the privilege of earning my living doing what I loved most. Not that there haven't been sad times. Over the past fifty years, I've lost a number of friends to aviation accidents. Sometimes the accidents were caused by carelessness or recklessness, but there were many pilots who were excellent craftsmen, like Dick Chamberlin and Duane Easterly of PNA, who hit a peak just east of Anchorage, Alaska, in 1960. All you can say about accidents like that is, "there, but for the grace of God, go I."

There are, in my opinion, three skills required to fly well. A pilot needs to know how to manipulate the controls to get the machine to do what he or she wants it to do. This requires a stimulus-response sort of learning, which, with practice, can get the majority of the population in and out of the air under reasonable conditions. Then there's the book learning—the ability to read and understand navigation, weather, regulations and aircraft systems. Finally, there is experience and good judgment, probably the most important element in developing the competency to handle a flying job.

It's been said that good judgment comes from having exercised bad judgment and gotten away with it. There are a number of times over the years that I have said to myself, "I don't have to do that twice to learn it's dumb or dangerous." If you listen well to other pilots when they talk about their experiences, you don't even have to do something once to know it's not good.

Having a mentor who speaks straight is also a first-rate protective device. My cousin Bob was that kind of mentor. He made sure that I learned the mechanics as well as the flying. And—something for which I am very grateful—he taught me a conservative approach to flying. There have been many times in my career when I have heard Bob's voice in my head saying, "Don't do foolish things." That persistent voice probably saved my life on more than one occasion.

Flying has been my passport to what has turned out to be a rich and satisfying life, peopled with very special men and women who have added to that richness. It's been a great adventure. You never know what's around the corner ... or over that next mountain.

Epilogue

Edward Wells ("Ted") Huntley
1930–1996

Ted Huntley was one of those rare individuals who never fell out of love with life. For him, there was always something exciting just around the next corner or over the next hill. Some new place to explore, some new idea to investigate.

In preparation for his retirement from Delta Air Lines, Ted purchased some vintage tugboats and launched a unique business that enabled him to feed his insatiable curiosity about all things scientific. He had the vision to recognize that the old vintage tugs with their wood hulls were perfect for housing the kind of sensitive electronic research equipment that universities, scientific organizations and the navy use in their marine research. So he set up a company to lease these vessels to these types of organizations. Since his clients' projects often required aerial support, the business also gave him a good excuse to keep flying.

In addition to flying, Ted also had a passion for mentoring and he did it in a way that truly empowered people. A neighbor of Ted's, Marsh Terry, a writer and marketing consultant, fondly remembers one of his experiences with Ted.

"Even at fifty-five I was a young pilot," Marsh recalls. " I only had 200 hours and was very, very leery of mountain flying. My idea of crossing the Cascades was to climb to 9,000 feet (2,700 m) and hold my breath for half an hour. Then Ted suggested we 'go up and take a peek,' as he would say when the weather was less than clear.

"We were going mountain flying. It was time I learned that piloting was more than just a safe, straight line from A to B. 'You must be aware of the wind,' Ted said as we entered Snoqualmie Pass, a major east-west thoroughfare through the mountain range that divides the state of Washington. 'Think of mountain flying as flying through a 'V.' If the wind is coming from the left of the 'V,' you fly on the right and vice versa. If you fly on the side of the 'V' the wind is coming from, it will push you down, whereas on the opposite side, it will be lifting you out. Also, you always want to leave yourself two escape routes (in mountain flying). Never just one. You'll want to be able to go left and out or down and out, or any combination of two potential exits.'

"As we flew between the peaks, the 'V' narrowed enough for me to voice concern that it didn't appear that we had enough room to turn 'around and out.' Ted said, 'Give me the plane.' He pulled the power back a bit, added a notch of flaps and easily maneuvered a figure eight in the space where I didn't think I could make an 'O.' 'You see,' he said, 'when you're just learning to fly, you have no relative depth perspective for anything other than up and down. You're not taught to fly near anything so you never learn the size of the circle your plane can turn within.' I learned a lot from that day, and I learned a lot from that man."

Ted's love of flying, mentoring and Alaska all came together in the work he did for the Alaskan Aviation Safety Foundation, a non-profit organization dedicated to making flying in Alaska safer. According to Tom Wardleigh, who spearheads the foundation, Ted joined the organization in 1985 and became one if its strongest supporters. He carried his message of safety throughout southeast Alaska, lecturing in Ketchikan, Wrangell, Petersburg, Sitka, Juneau, Fairbanks, Anchorage and Kenai ... always at his own expense. He did it because he believed that by sharing his experiences and what he had learned in his years of bush flying, he just might be able to save some young pilot's life.

In 1995, Ted was invited to Sweden to view a new technology: an airborne laser mapping system that combines laser range-finding, the Global Positioning System, computer processing and video imaging. With the laser's ability to "see" the ground beneath arid scrub vegetation and even through the dense canopy of an evergreen forest, this new technology provides a way to obtain terrain data under conditions that were previously considered impossible. Fired up by the potential he saw for the system, he put together investors to form a company that could put the technology to practical use in such areas as forest management, power line design and monitoring, mining exploration, and snowpack and glacier monitoring.

Ted seemed virtually unstoppable in his enthusiasm for this new venture, but on April 7, 1996—Easter Sunday— the unimaginable happened. Ted Huntley died of a massive heart attack. No one was ready to lose him, not his family, not his friends, not his business associates. Yet, in retrospect, I'm sure Ted died exactly as he would have wanted to. He was in Mississippi testing the new equipment for his latest venture. Because he was unable to get home for Easter, a group of his old flying buddies had flown in for a visit. When death came for Edward "Ted" Huntley, it found him surrounded by laughter, good friends and good food ... doing the thing he enjoyed most next to flying—swapping flying stories.

Index

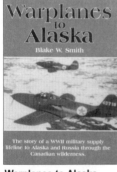